TACIT URBANISM

Hawkers and the production of space
in every day Kolkata

Christopher Dell
in collaboration with
Patrick S L Ghose

post editions, Rotterdam 2009

Contents

Urban Transformation

India is in the process of a fast-paced urbanisation. Indian cities among the top megacities in the world today are Mumbai, Chennai, Bangalore, Hyderabad and Kolkata, others will follow. Even medium-sized cities grow into metropolises. In India there are 35 cities today with a population of over one million. This boom stands simultaneously in contrast to the inequality between regions and the concentration of infrastructure in big cities. How are the economies in these cities driven? Which public, or semi-public spaces are cultivated by these cities?

The complexity of the urban situation of Indian cities shows the complex manner urbanisation runs its course. That means: when we look at the urban and its complex movements of space production, we can neither define cities as self-referencing container-objects, nor as examples of universal modernity. With the inclusion of the history of the city, it not only becomes clear how the urban does differentiate itself in many layers, movements, rhythms, conflicts and centres; what also becomes visible is then rising differentiation. New urban forms generate new socio-spatial relationships.

The urbanisation of India is organised in a net of complex configurations, and the aspects which unevenly articulate themselves. This unevenness is also moulded through economy, the social history of the country and specific forms of colonial, and the consequential post-colonial capitalism. Global economic processes have manifold effects on the urbanisation process in different regions. So the intertwining of global markets and local-regional politics is different in the cities, for example, of Delhi, Mumbai, Bangalore or Kolkata. This is a mutual process. Not only do international-capitalistic forms of the division of labour affect regional politics, local and national processes also do intervene and bring differentiations with them.

Urbanisation can thus be examined on global, national and

regional levels of concrete urban growth. This differentiation of levels helps to understand how, according to the respective focus and weightage, cities in India show very different levels of development. Even within these levels, complex and differentiated reciprocations meet one another.

So, for example during the analysis of migration patterns, it is not only economical grounds, but also infrastructural parameters like traffic and communication, and other topological-ecological factors, which vary space, specifically those that play a role in the development of cities. Urban growth can be created through caste-networks, which through their exclusion of accessibility in turn causes migration. The other way around, policy measures for infrastructure can support the new economies and migration to the city.

The (post) colonial city

Contemporary cities like Mumbai, Kolkata, Chennai, and later Delhi, grew out of colonial grounds. The complex, multifaceted dynamism of these cities can however only be understood if the pre-colonial history of the regions is taken into consideration. How do different modes of urban planning cooperate, and how do grids of the pre-colonial European city superimpose on pre-colonial city designs?

Colonial capitalism creates two types of cities. For one, the existing city configurations (*kasbas* and *ganj*) are intertwined with new city centres of international trade. Thus a direct juxtaposition of rational order in a European city is created, with military installations, administrative headquarters for the imperial economy, and on the other side, urban planning configurations, which are developed out of the growth of old city pathways. Other cities are newly created through infrastructural projects like ports or railway stations. Kolkata, Chennai or Mumbai can be counted as belonging to this type. These centres carry a trail of development of the hinterland with them, which spreads the growing organisation and connection of new cities, which have grown together into today's metropolitan regions. In the colonial phase, Indian cities were differentiated through clear-cut civil, as well as military lines. There evolved 'white' cities as well as those with the local population. Even in Kolkata, as in Mumbai and Chennai, these spatial allocations do superimpose on the city configuration. They differentiate themselves further in caste divisions, professional groups, and social status. The order of administrative buildings, living quarters and villas, reflect the power structures of colonial capitalism.

Thus socio-spatial segregation is more often than not a colonial export item: the division of space in a European city and a native-zone is the central urban planning principle of the 19th century. The strong rural connection of the natives serves as the argument to perceive them predominantly as working immigrants who reside only temporarily in the cities, while the colonial rulers are more used to the concept of order and permanent residency. In this type of 'zoning' the aspect of hygiene also plays a major role: centres had to be established where the colonial rulers could live free from the dangers of life in tropical areas.[1]

The English colonial rulers refused to equip the city quarters inhabited by Indians with even rudimentary canalisation and water supply. The local real estate owner elite benefitted greatly from this measure by renting out overstaffed houses with the lowest standards of hygiene and living for highly profitable prices. Together with military and administrative-technical measures, it can be seen how closely the colonial city is connected to those controlling techniques which emerged with the rise of the national states. On this basis, drastic interventions in local living forms, the construction of new types of settlements and the control of the daily life of the colonised subjects became legitimised. The colonial rulers, moulded by western aesthetics, conceptions of space and everyday social life, stigmatised traditional informal utilisation of

[1] Cochrane, Allen, *Administered Cities*, in: Pile/Brook/Mooney (pub.),Unruly Cities?, London 1999,P.302

space and organisation of it as disorderly and chaotic. Even today, decolonised metropolises in independent India are seen by Western urbanists as ungovernable. But only one who normatively carries over western concepts such as teleological development or civil society instead of looking at concrete specific movements, has this image of an irrational, urban India.

The (post) industrial city

The contrast between urban and rural regions cannot be clearly defined in India. In Europe's case, Marx described the passage from feudal to the capitalistic system as a conflict between the city and the country. In India this conflict is not that obvious. The working class in the cities has never given up its connection to the villages and their structures. Thus, the economies of the Indian cities have developed less from industries than from a great mass of workers in labour-intensive and service sectors. Thereby, it also follows that the conceptualisation of urbanisation has to be based on this urban-rural continuum and includes all its aspects: economic, social, as well as cultural.

The spatial consequence of this division of labour, as is characteristic for the pre-industrial to industrial phase in Europe, works differently in the Indian context. In Europe, in the phase of industrialisation, the cityscape is altered by economic, political, and cultural transformations, and the spatial structuring in the city is decided by zoning. In India however, where cities like Kolkata and Mumbai are being also industrialised to a certain degree, the urban city planning is marked by a mixture of regional economy, industrialisation, and colonial order.

Critique of the Concept of Informality

Rurbanisation and the informal sector

India's urbanisation not only has a city-country effect; urban life in turn is also penetrated strongly by rural elements. This means that the majority of the urban population does not find any secure industrial, or service-sector based jobs. For one, the industrial sector has shrunk in the face of globalisation, and secondly, the high-technology sector of the globally operating call-centre services are accessible only to a privileged few.

Despite this fact, the formal sector mostly plays the predominant role in analyses of the urban working situation. Jan Breman states: *for a long time, little if any attention was given to the economic activities and the incomes derived therefrom with which... the majority of the urban population has to try to make ends meet.*[2] Informality, as policy of everyday production and reproduction, intrudes like a blind spot in the interpretation of the city.

The concept of the "informal sector" was first introduced as a subject of debate by the labour scientist, Keith Hart[3] in 1971 and he described the informal sector as that section of urban workforce which drops out of the organised job market. The ILO, the International Labour Organisation, quickly acquired this topic and spread the concept of the informal sector as the promise of new forms of labour beyond formal patterns.

In the view of the ILO and the World Bank, the difference between formal and informal sectors is defined above all structurally. Following that, the ILO gives the interpretation, (one highly welcomed from the neo-liberal perspective), that the characteristics of the informal sector like flexibility, adapting to the production conditions and so on, are hindered by the advantaging and protection of the formal sector through national governments. Thus, a demand for the improvement of the conditions of the informal economy is deduced, which for one, plays directly into the hands of the stepping back of the state from its responsibilities, but secondly, also implies the end of discrimination in informal working conditions.

---

[2] Breman, Jan, *Dualistic Labour System?*, in: Patel/Deb(pub.), Urban Studies, New Delhi 2006, p.81

[3] Hart, Keith, *Informal Income Opportunities and Urban Employment in Ghana*, in: Jolly/de Kadt/ Singer/ Wilson (pub.), World Employment: Problem and Strategy, Harmondsworth 1973

Breman draws attention to the problematics of such a language strategy: behind the dichotomy of formal vs. informal stands a dualistic ideology which can hardly do justice to the totality of the urban, the complex layers, and relationship networks. The formal sector is described as wage labour in a permanent working relationship, as for example in factories, administrations or large service-based enterprises. Such workplaces are firstly part of a well-organised work structure. Secondly, work situations which are registered in public statistics, and thirdly, workplaces which are amenable to legal protection.

All economies which cannot be classified under this category are subsumed under the informal sector. Structure is turned around: it is not about dependent occupations, but independent work in its broadest sense. Independent work is hard to record and hence does not appear in public reports. And precisely because independence is so hard to define, reports about informal occupations consist mostly of undifferentiated listings of types of activities: petty traders, newspaper vendors, shoeshiners, etc. A large group of small enterprises which, with irregular incomes, move along the fringes of the urban economy.

Informal labour and space

The old picture of the city visualises urban industrialisation as a pattern of order, that as a dynamic centre, overcomes the rural disorders and offers stable working conditions.

In reality, it however looks as though the growth of regulated workplaces can in no way keep pace with the rapid rise in available manpower. The number of regulated workplaces decreases rather with the liberalisation and globalisation of the markets. So the informal sector becomes the collecting pool of those in the urban population who have no access to the highly productive "modern" urban sector.

It however would be false to imagine the informal sector as socially isolated and spatially dislocated. The highest percentage of the urban population today works in the informal sector. The hawkers on the streets of Kolkata are a clear example of how the informal sector moulds the cityscape and produces urban space. This example shows how the informal economies happen not only in the centre of the urban. Furthermore, it becomes clear that the activities of the hawkers are absolutely profitable, efficient, and very beneficial for the population. It also means that it is not so appropriate only to consider aspects of work management, when analysing the phenomenon, and thus quantify work processes as products only. It is much more appropriate to see the urban process as such: as more about the context in which people work, and on which they pattern themselves through their practices. The emphasis lies less in the form of the activity and more on the mode of production itself.

The informal reacts directly to the concrete needs and demands of the city quarters. Here more efficiency is achieved with low capital intensity and the simplest of methods.

And because it is a question of context and the hawkers operate in the middle of the city, the informal sector cannot be viewed as a completely separate economic unit. Formulated in another way: to press the urban system into a dualistic view of division would carry with it the danger of losing sight of the totality of the urban and its productive and reproductive relationships.

Less is known about the relation between informal labour and social stratification. One mostly starts with the premise that formal working relationships are accessible to trained manpower who are from a higher social milieu, while the informal sector consists of the uneducated, who are recruited from the lower social strata. This premise is highly superficial. The urban population in India is very heterogeneous. Studies about slums have shown, according to Breman, that these are neither reduced to a certain social order, nor do they deviate from the pattern of the total urban system.

Density Max

It is correct that the informal sector predominantly constitutes itself out of a rural migrant population. However, these are in the city for years and contribute to the structuring of new urban forms .

Thus it makes no sense to marginalise the rural influences and movements in the urban.

Rather a strong reciprocation comes into force. The massive rise in manpower through immigration constitutes the soul of urbanisation. It is not about direct physical movement but also about ways of production and organisation which percolate from the rural to the city and superimpose on the urban. Thus informal activities are on the upswing, while the migration from the country to the cities seems to be on the decline. Harold Lubell has determined in his study about Kolkata that the increase in population in the surrounding districts is slightly higher than in the urban agglomeration. According to Lubell, the country-city immigration in the last quarter of the 20th century has sharply declined, not only in West Bengal, but in the whole of India[4].

This could be a sign of the fact that the city centres have reached their maximum degree in density. Many informal workplaces are already assigned on a fixed basis. On the streets of Kolkata this urban saturation can already be seen: it is exceedingly difficult to find a place for a new vending stall.

The urban centre is not infinitely playable, nor infinitely compressible. It can rather be expanded spatially, it can coalesce into regions which overrun the rural, and without being influenced by the rural structures. The assumption that independent small enterprises and non-institutionalised activities can expand infinitely and newcomers could, with little know-how and means of production, take their place in the market, simulates a

---

[4] Lubell, Harold, *Urban Devolopment and Employment-The Prospects for Calcutta* , New York 1974

homogeneity that does not exist. Instead, conflict-laden situations constantly take place in the economy of urban space. There emerges a constant reciprocation of spatial order and social stratification.

Urban Involution – Proletariat of the Informal

In the informal sector, less jobs are created through division of labour than through the fragmentation of existing work. This also has the result of cutting up the income. Frederic Thomas describes the situation in Kolkata incisively: *three or four persons share an activity amongst themselves, which could easily be carried out by one of them, market women sit for hours before small towering fruit or vegetable stands; hairdressers, shoeshiners squat on the pavement for the entire day to serve only a handful of customers; small boys jump repeatedly right into the middle of the flowing traffic to sell paper handkerchiefs, to clean car windows, to offer magazines or single cigarettes; construction workers wait often in vain every morning in the hope of obtaining work*[5].

After the term Involution[6] was coined by Clifford Geertz in connection with rural developments in Java, city theoreticians of today like Thomas McGhee[7] and Mike Davies[8] talk increasingly about urban involution. By involution, Geertz understood the endeavour in the total system to find a niche for everyone, no matter how small it is. Urban involution can be characterised today by rapid urbanisation, chronic unemployment, and overpopulation. Rural traditions manifest themselves constantly in the city and open up a structure of occupations with minimum income.

---

[5] Thomas, Frederic, *Calcutta Poor: Elegies on a city above pretense*, Armonk 1997, p.114

[6] Geertz, Clifford, *Agricultural Involutiom: The Process of Ecological Change in Indonesia*, Berkeley 1963

[7] McGhee, Thomas, *Beachheads and Enclaves*, in: Yeung/Lo (pub.), Changing South-East Asian Cities : Readings in Urbanization, London 1976

[8] Davies, Mike, *Planet der Slums*, Berlin 2007

Debates about the informal sector often start with the assumption that urban production is an independent area of the national economy. In reality however, it is so that the urban and rural markets interact on the local level, mix, and thus strongly merit a regional point of view. It is also important not to overestimate the view on the urban as spatial order and density: in analysis, the circulation of work according to the seasonal rhythms is important.

That is why we should be less concerned about the division of the urban and the rural, and more about the interaction in these areas and their modes of production.

Difference

It becomes clear that the dualism of nice and neatly separated economies cannot be upheld. Different ways of production, distribution and consumption superimpose and converge in the urban system. The components influence each other and interact, so that we can see the urban economy only as a totality. Instead of starting from the binary opposition formal vs. informal, it would be, so says Jan Breman, better to speak of variously differentiated production relations which reveal themselves in different variations and gradations[9].

As Henri Lefèbvre makes clear in *The Production of Space*[10], the urban is to be understood as a totality of actions as social spatialisation. The concept of the informal sector sees itself confronted with the problem, that informal activities cannot be seen as isolated from the urban economy. Urban economy unifies different modes of production with corresponding production relations within itself. The differentiation of the urban system for the economy means that new ways of production and distribution can establish themselves without crystallizing themselves as isolated elements. It becomes clear that the strategy of demarcating certain

---

[9] Breman, Jan, *Dualistic Labour System?*, in : Patel/Deb (pub.), New Delhi 2006, p.92

[10] Lefèbvre, Henri, *Production of Space*, Oxford 1991

working relations serves the purpose of upholding certain monopolies in times of work shortage and narrow accessibility.

In this context, it cannot be let out of sight that the informal sector is not free of norms. On the contrary, it is permeated with social regulations which approach the level of contractual or semi-contractual ties.

Independence is, in this context, a relative term. For the majority of the urban population, informal work does not necessarily mean independent activity. They are tied into a complex network of dependencies. In the differentiated sub-markets of the urban economy, work becomes a fluid term.

Kolkata Case

Since India's independence, Kolkata has taken a special role among Indian metropolitan cities. The city did not succeed in upholding its dominance from colonial times and, unlike the other Indian metropolises of Mumbai, Delhi and Bangalore, to attract new industries. On the contrary, foreign as well as domestic capital left the city. Large-scale production grew after 1948 for a short-lived period, which then stagnated and finally began to lessen further and further. Rakesh Mohan has, in one of his analyses, investigated the relationships between production, occupation and urbanisation for the whole of India. He incidentally observes West Bengal as a *most striking case of deindustrialisation since Independence, with consistently low rates of urban-rural growth differential... At the time of Independence, industrial productivity of West Bengal was about 2.5 times the national average. Now it is about the same as the national average. Urban growth has been correspondingly low.*[11] West Bengal experienced an increase in its share of the gross national product by 18% in the year 1961, only to drop to 13% in 1971 and below 10% in 1981.

During colonial times Kolkata could not establish any local class of capital. Bengali capital was only in rare cases able to control the economy. Foreign capital, as well as producers from western India decided industry and trade trends in Kolkata. True, the city profited, as did Mumbai, from the first phase of industrialisation at the beginning of the 20th century. However, while in Mumbai a locally resident capitalist class pulled the strings, most of the industries in Kolkata were driven by English and Marwari capital. Soon after Independence, large parts of this capital were taken away from Kolkata. This resulted in the city losing its role as the most important urban centre of India and thereby the possibilities of influencing political decisions at the national level diminished likewise. The

---

[11] Mohan,Rakesh, *Urbanization in India. Patterns and Emerging Policy Issues*, in: Patel/Deb (publ.), *Urban Studies*, New Delhi 2006, p.78

frustration of the elite of West Bengal over this development consequently led them to thwart all attempts by non-Bengalis to establish themselves in politics. So capitalistic interests were blocked from the political level, whereas in other Indian metropolises they worked hand in hand.

This political inability to act, coupled with high migrant influx and economic opportunism, led to stagnation. Industrial diversification and modernisation bypassed Kolkata.

Migration: Rural and Refugee

Due to the precarious economic condition there was hardly any scope for new manpower to prosper in Kolkata. That is why small-scale economic activities gained in importance and became the dominant mode of production. The intensity of the informal economy increased simultaneously with the marked decrease in 'formal', socially secure workplaces.

Two factors ensured, despite economic stagnation, a great increase in the working population of Kolkata. On one hand, with the continuous urban-rural tension, the manpower of small trade recruited itself, besides the city-based population, from the surrounding towns and villages. The influx of rural elements makes the differentiation between what is rural and what is urban more and more difficult. Cities like Kolkata expand along communication-corridors, becoming extended metropolitan regions, after which the surrounding land regions *experience a change in their function and occupational situation in situ*, says the geographer David Drakakis-Smith, *changes that in turn retroact upon the urban centres*[12].

At the informal sector it exemplifies itself how the connection and intertwining of the urban and the rural lead to a sort of ruralisation.[13]

---

[12] Drakakis-Smith, David, *Third World Cities*, London 2000

[13] for further reading: Safa, Helen I., *Towards a political Economy of Urbanization in the Third World countries*, New Delhi 1982

Practices of the rural population show and transform themselves into the sidewalk economy, and grow into the city.

The other factor for the increase in manpower was the partitioning of India in the year 1947, which brought migrants from Pakistan to India. Later, the secession of Bangladesh in 1971 led to a great migrant movement from that country to India, and above all Kolkata. The immigrant families were often excluded from the regular economy and could only work in the informal sector. Their businesses usually remained in the family, being directly handed over to the next generation.

Sidewalk economies

According to the economist Nandini Dasgupta, petty trading/hawking is Kolkata's fastest growing economic branch.[14] A study made by the Alliance of Street Vendors of India assumes that more than 75% of the manpower in Kolkata is active in the informal sector.[15] Low investment rates, high unemployment rates and an economic standstill create the condition for small trade activities. Thus one can observe a substantial increase in street trading over the last few decades. With the increase in the density of trade, the hawkers spread throughout the city in spite of functional zoning and quarter-specific differences.

The number of hawkers in Kolkata rose between 1961 and 1972 by 186 percent. According to Dasgupta, about 100,000 people in 1981, and more than 150,000 people today are employed in this sector. The total number of those engaged in street trade rises once again, if micro-industries which provide for the markets are also considered . Many of the products, above all clothing but also household goods, are manufactured in home-based or small-scale industries.

[14] from: Dasgupta, Nandini , *Capital, the State, and Petty Trading in Calcutta*, in: Patel/Deb (pub.), Urban Studies, New Delhi 2006, P. 161-178

[15] Bhowmik, Sharit K., *Hawkers in the Urban Informal Sector: A study of street vendors in six cities*, National Alliance of Street Vendors of India.http://www.nasvinet.org

The labour scientist Sharit K.Bhowmik explains the process of hawking in very simple terms: *whoever gets no other job, becomes a hawker. To be a hawker means to take matters into one's own hands and not to wait till the State helps. This section of the urban poor tries to solve their problems through their own meagre resources. Unlike other sections of the urban population they do not demand that government create jobs for them, or engage in begging, stealing or extortion. They try to live their life with dignity and self-respect through hard work.*[16]

Bhowmik sees four factors at the core of the complex of the street vendor. First, the fact that street trade is classified as illegal by the authorities. Kolkata is the only city which does not issue licences for street trading. This practice is supported by legislation.

As per the Kolkata Municipal Corporation Act of 1980, hawking in Kolkata is governed by the communal administration. This law prohibits any form of street trade. In 1997, the West Bengal government suggested a sharper extension to section 371 of the Kolkata Municipal Corporation Act. The addition declared street trade as tantamount to illegal activity. Offences were to be punishable by law with imprisonment for upto three months or an amount of rupees 250. In relation to the illegal encroachment of public space the law explains: *it has been decided to declare any such encroachment by the hawkers, stall holders and other organisations as cognisable and non-bailable offence.*[17]

This leads directly to the second problem: the city planning. Public space for the communal city planners is only defined as parks, gardens, markets, hospitals, or educational institutions. Street trade is neither defined nor taken into consideration. The policy which resulted from over years of such a view was not in a position

---

[16] .ibid

[17] .ibid

to grasp the complexity of the actual socio-economic processes. Footpaths as open public space are the only option for people without access to the formal job market. When access to free spaces is restricted through city planning, options are lost, existence is threatened. Next, hawkers cannot work anywhere else than on the streets; and so, the inhabitants are dependant on the petty traders and use their services in everyday life.

Bhowmik observes that in this context the pressure on the hawkers also increases in and through the public. NGOs, which represent the elite,[18] begin to step in for cleaner cities. They argue aggressively for restoring the footpaths and their cleaning. Complaints about blocked streets, annoyance in public space find good resonance in the media. And this regularly leads to local and regional governments trying to bring order again in the city planning by prompting large-scale clean-ups.

But pressure also comes from the police and the gangs. According to a study by NASVI the rental charges for street trading have increased sharply. Hawkers must give away between 10% to 20% of their income as protection money. In Mumbai alone, 4 billion rupees in protection money is paid annually.

Bhowmik sees the question about the consumers, the users as the third factor. Who buys from the hawkers? What advantages and disadvantages do consumers see in street trading?

Nearly all classes buy from hawkers. 82% of the consumers buy their food daily from them. The upper class buys, due to taste, their food from special traders. The middle class provides itself here with clothing, vegetables and fruits. The greatest share however, comes from the city's poor. They buy on the street, because supermarket prices are beyond their means.

---

[18] One example is the NGO called PUBLIC (people united for better living in calcutta), who is represented, among others, by Bonani Kakkar. An interview with her can be found on page 88.

In conclusion, the factors of legislation, city planning and consumers' view for Bhowmik cumulate in the fourth and final point: the demand to analyse and rate street vending in its totality.

Socio-ethnic Diversity

Hawkers are not to be equated with the poor. Many of the petty traders and small entrepreneurs earn a comparatively good income. Even the sociologist Jan Breman differentiates between the petit-bourgeoisie and the sub-proletariat.[19] Dasgupta also confirms that the petty trading sector absorbs manpower from all segments of the socio-ethnically complex, assembled job market. This complexity is also connected to the fact that Kolkata, as narrated in the beginning, has a long and intense history of migration. After the partition, refugees from higher and well-educated classes as well, fled to Kolkata. Besides that, people from the surrounding districts try to find work in Kolkata. That means a section of the petty traders has limited or no education and can most easily earn a livelihood in the informal sector. There is also a section of traders which, due to the downfall of industry, has switched from the formal to the informal sector. According to a study by Sharit K.Bhowmik[20], 22% of all hawkers in Kolkata alone were previously engaged in the formal sector.

Hawkers assemble themselves from different classes and ethnicities. 6% have a high school degree. To be a hawker does not necessarily mean to belong to the lower class, to be poor. Petty trade is for most of them a relatively good source of income, a "fixed" workplace. Hawkers earn between Rs 40 and Rs 80 a day. They work for over 10 hours a day however, under the most difficult circumstances and under the constant threat of removal. Fifty percent of the hawkers with higher education, who were also born in the city, constitute the second generation of migrants from

---

[19] from: Patel/Deb (publ.), *Urban Studies*, New Delhi 2006,p. 27

[20] Bhowmik, Sharit K., *Hawkers in the Urban Informal sector: A study of street vendors in six cities*, National Alliance of Street Vendors of India. http://www.nasvinet.org

Bangladesh. Even though the share is not yet exorbitant, it however shows how sections of the middle class drift towards the lower income sector. According to an inquiry, it was almost impossible for newcomers to the city in the 1970's, to find employment, apart from petty trading. 41% of those questioned said that they had no alternative, 26% felt it to be the easiest solution, and 17% knew someone who already worked in that sector.

These observations point to the importance of the production relationships. Immigrants prefer target areas where they already know people who help them to shoulder the heavy entry costs during shifting base to the urban space. Mediators from the respective social-ethnic groups establish contact with the producers, wholesalers and middlemen for financial matters.

Conversely, a steady pool of new manpower is opened up for the wholesellers. Advantages of social ties in this context also create dependencies. According to Abdul Naziz[21], this socio-economic factor is more decisive for the attraction of the city than the difference in wages, as was previously assumed. This explains why it is possible that Kolkata, despite a limping formal economy and high unemployment rate, continues to attract immigrants.

Socio-ethnic connections are an advantage and every social-ethnic group or subgrouping, seeks to influence the mechanism, by promoting its people.

Spatial Structures

Even though global markets are settling in Kolkata, economy and spatial structure of the city remain largely untouched. The same automobiles drive through the streets honking non-stop as they did thirty years before, traffic collapse is a permanent condition.

A high percentage of Kolkata's population has no access to proper

---

[21] Aziz,Abdul, *Urban Poor and Urban Informal Sector,* Columbia 1984

housing. They exist in intermediate spaces, also on the streets, and the footpaths are almost constantly occupied.

They have invented their own economy and culture of survival They live under plastic coverings, in shacks, constructions whose walls consist of recyclable material. The workplace is at the dwelling entrance, or under staircases, highway driveways, or just attached parasitically to existing living or business quarters. Whole production units are located out in the open.

It is not only cheaper to buy from hawkers than in the supermarkets, the distances are shorter too. Everyone buys from the street peddlers right at their doorstep, have their snacks on the way, and even have a shave or a haircut. There unfolds a semi-public space in between, which though informal, is thoroughly organised. Every space is allotted to a fixed person; gangs as well as police regularly encash their "hafta", the bribe money. Some live in their informal shops, some commute home at night and return the following morning. This movement alone of workers in the early morning and late evening, creates intense traffic.

These intermediate spaces are architecturally a steady fixture of the cityscape. Many installations are so large that it is almost impossible to move along the pavement. Production of space here is direct: the pavement lives from public-cum-private space of the hawkers and their activities. Structure and creation of space of the informal sector thus remains integral to the city and preserves their specific characteristics. The informal sector fans itself out from technically advanced to completely rudimentary tasks. The asymmetric integration of technology creates an imbalance in the distribution of infrastructural and constructional environments in the city.

Sidewalk Typology

There is no set rule on how to build a stall. Everyone builds a structure for himself from which he can offer his work and his products. Thereby different types of constructions are created, which are partially canopied, partially open, partly stationary, partly mobile. Stationary units are packed up overnight, goods and tools remaining there. Canopies are docked to conveniently available structures like garden fences and lampposts.

Many of the shops unite themselves into a hybrid mixture of utilities and functions: *small pan-shops which offer betel leaves to chew act also as informal savings banks and furniture agencies.*[22] Different types of stands evolve, which through their construction can be traced back to their utilities: motorcycle workshops, fruit vendors, newspaper sellers, writers who sit at a typewriter and type letters, applications, fills out forms for illiterate customers, as well as hairdressers, restaurants on carts, or laundries. Religion too is provided for - temples are to be found on the footpaths, sometimes with, sometimes without personnel.

Local Governance, city planning and blind field

The colonial city and indigenous settlements were the antipodes of the colonial era in which the European order as being urbanistic was the thesis, and the mixed-up structure of local forms of settlement, the antithesis. This was portrayed and separated in the city spaces clearly. Today the antithesis cuts right through the city. This also contributes to the fact that the centre does not waste away despite economic stagnation: hawkers enliven the urban space and create local socio-economic relationships. The footpath becomes the field of production, reproduction and negotiation for the necessities and living habits of the users, and in turn is remodelled gradually by these usages.

The extreme density of Kolkata leads to unusual traffic patterns. People try to find a possible short-cut path to work. Most of them go on foot, because the major hindrance in Kolkata is transport.

---

[22] CRIT , *Urban Foam Bubbles(Urbane Schaumblasen)* , in: archplus 185, November 2007 , p.43

Spending the night on the footpath is not a rarity, if it serves to bring the workplace nearer.

To the majority of the population, private vehicles are not affordable and even if they were, the streets of Kolkata only offer 6% of the total area (compared to 25% on an average in European metropolises). The extremely dense city space promotes other usages. Hawkers ensure, by densifying the city structures even further, that for many inhabitants basic needs are made available within walking distance. That also means: the poor live directly beside the rich.

A relocation of hawkers would carry with it a plus in traffic. Vice-versa a higher traffic flow needs a new infrastructure. Firstly there is hardly any public money available for it, and secondly, such infrastructural measures would cut back public space even further.

Experience shows that large-scale solutions always carry newer problems with them. Every street or rail construction project necessitates the relocation of a large number of people. It mostly hits the poorer sections of the population. They then are in no position to offer their services in the city, or if they are, do so under very difficult circumstances.

Thus petty trading has not only economic but also city-spatial implications. Intense conflicts regarding urban space take place in the city centres and in most important economic nodal points. Prices of legalised living space per square metre by far exceed the annual income of the hawkers. The possibility of livelihood not only forces the settlement of businesses in the city, but also proximity to the workplace to minimise costs and time. As a logical consequence, the footpaths are completely occupied. Practically all gaps left during the building of the city are immediately filled with informal stands, which often serve as shelters as well. Thus the occupying actors behave in an economically reasonable way, without needing any planning. They use the available space as the situation demands. The footpath becomes not only the instrument for the movement of pedestrians, but also the free ground for survival strategies. Users interpret the city directly as a resource, by which socially integrating relations are created in the usage automatically. The corners of traffic ways become superimposed with a new mixture of usages, and in a permanent process of adaptation, are understood as an open urban infrastructure.

As the economy of the pavement, petty trade leads to a reorganisation of the city spaces right from the bottom up. In the space of a short period of time spatial acquisitions are created, constructional occupations of the footpath in public space, without any kind of planning from above. In the intermediate space directly in front of the villas and dwellings of the residents , an intermediate city is created which cuts through the centre in the most manifold of ways and where the major part of the population finds employment. The categories of public and private have little significance here; they turn out to be below complex.

That means, city planning is far removed from reality. For planning reduces itself to the physical treatment of space; social, cultural and economic concerns play no role whatsoever. City planning assumes that there is no informal economy, while over 50% of the population is active in this sector. So it officially allots no space for hawkers and thus neglects everyday practice.

While current city government officially blanks out the real circumstances in public debates regarding city planning, it simultaneously utilises the conditions in the form of protection money and manipulations in the election process. Profits are made from that which does not exist officially. Thereby the pressure is increased on those who go about their livelihood without having any rights. Propaganda trials and cleanup drives are not oriented towards any solution, and on the contrary, they only serve to distract from the real, existing problems, and intensify the discrimination against those who need protection.

Instead of restrictive measures, it should be demanded of the governments to pursue a policy of animation and assistance to the informal activities, as for example, the allocation of small credits, further education, infrastructural assistance, provision of materials, as well as the containing of mafia-centric structures and protection money payments. Stimulating small-scale activities makes sense alone due to the fact that the contribution of the informal sector to the producing force in the city is enormous, and above all, provides the poor with affordable goods.

Eviction-policy also doesn't make much sense, because the informal sector doesn't restrict itself to the streets alone, but is integrated into a widely enmeshed net of economies dependent on each other. A study by Amitava Bose[23] shows how formal and informal markets are also intertwined. The growth of dominating producers is coupled with the judicial weakness of informal structures. Large manufacturers use the small units in order to operate in additional market segments. The other way around, employment opportunities are created through this mechanism for those who have no access to the legal job market. Bose sees the inequality of the sectors as related to the colonialistic system, by which, not only economic surplus is deducted but also capital, what iwould otherwise be used for the subsistence of production conditions.

Thus urban segregation is not a static problem, but a socio-political field of conflict about space, in which city planning under the premise of city beautification and progress on the one hand intensifies economic competition; and on the other hand often robs the informal settlers of the very basic foundation for their existence. Thus in communist Kolkata of 1996 *occupants were driven from the centre to the city's outskirts, to be evicted one more time, as places had to be created for the newly built settlements of the middle*

---

[23] Bose, Amitava, *The Informal Sector in the Calcutta Metropolitan Economy*, ILO, WEP/WP , Genf 1974
[24] Davies,Mike, *Planet of Slums*, Berlin 2007,p.109

class.[24] City planner Ananya Roy states that *the territorial settlement border of the Kolkata region is meanwhile being marked by an inexorable cycle of colonisation, eviction and renewed colonisation.*[25]

City cleaning is justified as an essential means to fight crime, but it is also about forming homogeneous socio-economic areas in the city, which can allegedly be controlled more efficiently. Fundamental restructuring of urban space through aggressive city planning seeks to reduce the diversity that plays itself out in the centre of Kolkata.

A Small History of City Beautification

Political confrontrations in the city about the spatial extension of hawkers reach back to the 1970s. At the beginning of the 70s, the aggregation of footpaths has assumed such proportions that the state government and the city authorities see themselves forced to act. The attempt to enforce the eviction of the petty traders from public space is however prevented through stiff resistance by the local traders.

By 1975 the number of hawkers has increased extremely. The city administration speaks of the fact that Kolkata is choked with petty traders. Hawkers, as unauthorised occupants of public space, are on the one hand interpreted as a source of harassment for the pedestrians, and on the other, aesthetic pollution of the cityscape.

The situation culminates in "Operation Hawkers", the first largely applied eviction drive for the removal of hawkers from city space. However during this cleanup action city quarters were not treated equally. While business districts are clamped down upon, the areas Sealdah, Shyambazar and Baghbazar are spared from evictions. Here the hawkers have already organised themselves into unions.

[25.] Roy,Ananya , The *Gentleman's City : Urban Informality in the Calcutta of New Communism*, in :Syyad /Roy, *Urban Informality* , Lanham 2004, p.159

Areas in the vicinity of hospitals, where because of hygienic grounds hawkers create a genuinely problematic situation, remain untouched. Due to the unequal treatment of the districts, the suspicion soon dawns on everyone that the evictions have less to do with the interests of city development and more to do with protecting the interests of wholesalers who want to get rid of the competition. "Operation Hawkers" had to be given up quickly. Protests came not only from social relief organisations, but also from residents themselves, who for long had got used to the service complex right at their doorstep and learned to value its advantages. With the change from the Congress Party to the Left Front government in 1977, a laissez-faire politics was adopted against the hawkers, which however did not really address any problems. The promise to stick up for the poor population is very soon replaced by the focus on getting votes of the privileged class. Frederic Thomas describes the dilemma thus : *Lip service is paid repeatedly for the benefit of the poor, but the lion's share of the household in Kolkata serves to satisfy the needs of the middle- and upper-classes. Only ten percent of the budget of the city planning authorities is set aside for the renovation of bustees.*[26]

In 1996, the state of West Bengal starts the greatest campaign ever made against street traders. The drive is being spearheaded by the minister for transport in West Bengal who makes his tenure in office dependent on the success of the eviction drive. The government decrees the Kolkata Municipal Corporation Act, which categorises all activities of hawkers in public space as a criminal act that can be punished by imprisonment.

The mayor of Kolkata tries to ease the law by proposing to relocate the hawkers in market halls specially prepared for them. But this proposal is not accepted. "Operation Sunshine" begins on the night of 24 November 1996. 10,000 policemen, members of the Left

---

[26] Thomas, Frederic, *Calcutta Poor:Elegies on a City above Pretense*, Armonk 1997 , p.147

Front as well as private security forces demolish1640 stands and arrest 102 hawkers at Shyambazar. In the nightly drive afterwards more than 7,000 hawkers are removed from the footpaths of Hatibagan and Gariahat.

The Hawker Sangram Committee[27] is founded as a direct reaction to Operation Sunshine. The association stands in the centre of the opposition against the city government. HSC tries to sensitise the public to the problems, organises events, protest marches, strikes, signature campaigns, and street blockades. This results in widespread public opposition against Operation Sunshine. The drive is ceased. Still, the situation for hawkers remains very precarious.

On the 9th of February 2002, the Times of India[28] reports that the communist government of Kolkata speaks of intensifying the Kolkata-wide action against those hawkers who erect permanent or semi-permanent stalls. The CMC conservancy team of the city pulls down 500 unauthorised structures in the BBD Bag area in its nightly drives; Strand Road, Kiran Sankar Ray Road, Lyons Range follow later. Mayor Subrata Mukherjee is willing to enforce the cleaning of the city at any cost. He wants however, so the newspaper says, to avoid any public reactions.

Provoked by the pressure of trade unions, the National Policy for Urban Street Vendors is ratified by the Indian government as the regulating plan for the informal sector. The Kolkata municipality proposes in February 2004 to legalise hawkers. The city wants, so says the Times of India[29], to equip hawkers with identity cards. Not averse to profiting from it, the municipality wants 100 Rupees from

---

[27] The HSC is the umbrella organisation of 25 hawker unions in Kolkata. Its example shows how the informal job market is organised in parts. Hawkers can align with each other into unions, NGOs like the NASVI also engage themselves politically for the rights and interests of the hawkers.

[28] *CMC intensifies drive against hawkers*, Times of India , 9. 2.2002

[29] *ID cover for hawkers*, Times of India, 19.2.2004

the street traders per annum. The building laws too undergo a new regulation: up to a third of the footpaths can be used for trade, however no permanent constructions can be erected. Further, no informal settlements will be permitted at crossings within a radius of 50 metres. For food peddlers there is a hygiene plan: plastic gloves and clean clothes shall be distributed. However, the implementation moves forward slowly and the Kolkata Municipal Corporation - KMC, continues to deal harshly with the hawkers. *Money from hawkers but the civic body penalises the poor instead of the police sergeants,* says Shaktiman Ghosh, one of the union leaders.[30]

A complete dialectic of a tacit urbanism between formal and informal unfolds itself. Behind the backdrop, fights take place concerning something which really exists, but is simultaneously faded out and negated in public perception.

In November 2007, the Times of India[31] reported about the new plans of the municipality regarding the subject of hawkers. There will be a cleaning that in its scale will beat Operation Sunshine. In the course of Operation Sunshine there were 7,000, this time it is 10,000 hawkers who will be affected. On the 21st of January 2008 however nothing has happened so far. An article in The Telegraph headlines:*Kick-start to hawker ouster.*[32] The CMC affirms once again to enforce the new *hawker policy* with immediate effect.

Violence and the Tacit City

The city theoretician Thomas Sieverts tries to define the heterogeneous movements of the urban in the mode of an intermediate city: *in all cultures of the world they have the same specific characteristics: a structure made from totally different urban*

---

[30] *Chased out and back, for hawkers it's life as usual*, Indian Express, 12.9.2007

[31] *KMC plans mega eviction drive*, Times of India, 30.11.2007

[32] *Kick-start to hawker ouster*, Telegraph, 21.1.2008

milieus, which at first glance appears diffuse and disorganised, penetrated with separate, geometrically structured islands, a structure without a definite centre, but therefore with many more or less strongly specialised quarters, networks and nodal points.[33] Sieverts however overlooks the conflict-laden confrontations regarding space in the centre on the one hand, and the fights between urban spaces regarding central functions within the city structure on the other. In these conflicts centres can change, they can move in cities, which becomes clear from the phenomenon of gentrification. It is precisely in the attempts at city cleaning that it crops up which centres should be protected and which should be left to the informal market.

The situation is permanently precarious: traders are tolerated, act however in a space free of laws. Hawkers need space for their work. The fact that they have no legal access to it raises for them the question concerning the right to the city, the right to land and physical space in the urban a constant subject. What rights do those have, who care for, preserve, use and enliven space?

As in other metropolitan cities in India, the local order of violence structures itself at the breaking point between legality and legitimacy. Violence, or the threat of violence, is omnipresent in this urban space. Blackmail and the protection economy expand and are maintained through the participation of gangs. In the late 70's, mafia alliances, previously part of the smuggling trade, turn to the real estate and housing market. In the complex interplay of politics, NGOs, police and mafia, a hardly visible net is created, a tacit net of control of the informal market. This tacit net creates and strengthens a culture of fear and dislocation. Space organisation is interlaced by the driving actors with the control of informal processes of power.[34]

Informality in this context does not imply the absence of the State.

---

[33] Sieverts, Thomas, *Cities without centers*, London 2003, p.3

State authorities like the police and municipality profit from the illegality of the informal. The State is absent only in matters of infrastructure, social services and security of law. Public land and ground, as for example the footpaths, are not controlled by the space planning authorities, but by a community of interests comprising city officials, policemen and gangs. For the footpath inhabitants this means to pay money for a protectorate. This is on what the power of gangs is based, who without any formal rights, lease places to hawkers, and also on their connection with the authorities and politicians to whom they sell the votes of the tenants in exchange for their protection. As the whole process is illegal, demands are characterised by informal requests and not the demand for rights.

City of users, City of mixed functions

City planning concepts stigmatise, criminalise and marginalise informality. In order to recognise the actual struggles in an urban city increasingly marked by the capitalistic logic of exploitation, the practices of the local actors cannot be reduced to mere survival strategies. Such a perspective distorts the view on the complex social, cultural and political relationships in the city arrangement and its base economy. Therefore city researchers Solomon Benjamin and Bhuvaneshwari Raman propose the term *occupative urbanism*[35] which takes into view the city of users.

The colonisation of the footpaths is a complex process of

[34.] *Corruption, in the form of bribery and extortion, ate into the earnings of these people and further reduced their income. In normal circumstances, street vendors part with 10 to 20% of their earnings to local authorities as bribes. During times when eviction drives are undertaken by the municipal authorities, the bribes increase considerably. At these times street vendors pay larger sums to corrupt officials to forewarn them of impending raids. It would appear that these periodic eviction drives are carried out mainly to increase the rents sought by these officials.* In: Bhowmik, Sharit K., *Hawkers in the Urban Informal Sector: A study of street vendors in six cities*, National Alliance of Street Vendors of India. Http:// www.nasvinet.org

[35.] Benjamin,Solomon,Raman,Bhuvaneshwari, *Occupative Urbanism*, in: archplus 185 , November 2007

appropriation of space. The multiple structure of possessions permit the unfolding of an individual economic structure in the micro-settlements. *The apparently chaotic possession and utilisation relationships* and the absence of planning paradoxically create a basis for the circumstance that *land is upvalued at a radical rate*.[36] At a closer glance the various ground relationships reveal themselves. Some stalls are only temporary, others are arranged for constant use by the traders.

In this context, it becomes important to analyse the culture of utilisation of space as well as the development of housing/business constructions by the users. A construction project, whatever it may be, cannot be seen as an isolated object, but is to be understood only in the context of a social-spatial reality which includes the constructional structure, the living form and the urban practices. Exchange of goods is not only to be reduced to the economy, but is also a cultural activity, the production of space.

The anthropologist Amos Rapoport proposes three different categories for the analysis of the utilisation of space: firstly the cultural, secondly the social, and thirdly, behaviour-related space.

1. Cultural space is described by Rapoport as: *space defined by different groups affected by training, previous experience, adaption, memory and cognitive categories of the group.*[37]

The limitations of the market through economic as well as social factors do not give hawkers the opportunity to buy or rent land. Instead they have founded a new form of constructional possession on the open terrain of the footpath. Simultaneously cultural differences also lead to the fact that for a large number of people it is not possible to get formal workplaces. Therefore they design self-sufficient models of working which offer little security

[36] Benjamin,Solomon,Raman, Bhuvaneshwari, *Occupative Urbanism*, in: archplus 185, November 2007

[37] Rapoport, Amos, *House Form and Culture* , New Jersey 1969,

but provide an income and thus a new culture of production.

Another cultural factor is that the streets in their dimensions were not planned for hawkers in the first place. The spatial dimensions are in no way tuned to the activities that occur on the street. Water supply, electricity and other infrastructural components are either not available, or are parasitically tapped into from the public and private net. Thus here it is not that the individual resident unit gets the supply, instead everyone must endeavour to get access at an informal level, and organise themselves to get at the means. The municipality can also earn underhand: when it closes both eyes as when water or electricity lines are tapped, or buildings are extended.

2. Behaviour-oriented space *is space which is available as a behaviour setting of a given individual or group.* Hawkers play a central role in the entire housing complex, in the daily life of the residents. Not too many residents shop in the supermarket or in the speciality store: they are either much too expensive or too far away - an important point in Kolkata, as movement of traffic is extraordinarily time-consuming. Everyone buys directly from in front of their residence, procure their daily necessities from the immediate resident petty traders. Resident and hawker form an occupational community within which their work and social relationships superimpose on each other. The interesting thing is that social interaction does not play itself out layer-specifically in private, but in the open, which is an inner space at the same time: as temporary living space of the hawkers. That also means for example that one sits as a customer out in the open when one has a shave. Cars and motorcycles are not only parked but also serviced, repaired and guarded. One sees another for lunch.

3. All these spaces can be subsumed under the term 'social'. Rapoport however sees very specific components: *social space as the spatial arrangements reflecting the patterns and regularities of*

various social groups, their hierarchies and roles. The social function of the footpaths and their spatial structuring has social-hierarchic components. They have however, other than constructionally planned arrangements in the city, not been created out of formal zoning, but have resulted from the job market for migrants and the informal economy created as a result therefrom.

This means that here social forms do intermix. For example, hawkers in villa quarters are directly integrated into the social culture. When the monsoon arrives and it is hardly possible to exist on the streets, hawkers are requested to move into the house corridor to stay there for a transitional period.

Urban Production of Space

Urban cultural production of space encompasses several practices that comprise the organisation of immediate needs, the reproduction of production and production relationships. The sectors of food, clothing, habitation as well as production in public space, create their own specific forms and mould the urban. So the hawkers are also a central component of the production of space, individual as well as a community. The political is embedded in these practices, in open and invisible forms and representations of dominance and resistance.

Urban culture is decided through the density, size of the urban and its demographic factors. Conversely, the spatial organisations of the forms of habitat and their transformations also have their effects on the city structure. Spatial practices of the cultural restrict themselves not to the artistic, but also include production, distribution and exchange of foodstuffs on the street, as well as the hairdressing stalls, laundries or typing services for the illiterate and the creation of living space like stalls, huts. These are arranged in the art and manner of how citizenry develops, is defined, and acquired.

The example of Kolkata shows how economic production

conditions play a role not only for the capital but also for the informal sector. It also becomes clear how economic systems influence urban space.

City planning that thinks and acts in an integrated manner should find new ways.

One has to think in terms of multi-scale: to differentiate between that which should be planned centrally, and what measures should be made ready for unforeseen activities and transformation of open structures. That also means: the urban is not to be interpreted as the final product, but as a political negotiating ground of its real users.

Inside/Outside: questioning neutral space

Nothing exists without exchange, without union, without proximity, that is, without relationships. The city creates a situation, the urban situation, where different things occur one after another and do not exist separately but according to their differences. ~ Henri Lefèbvre.

In the spectrum of the global, post-liberal metropolis, the pavement economies exhibit a space at which the borders of citizen and non-citizen, civil order and disorder, the legitimate and the illegitimate are constantly (re)defined and negotiated. Although the neo-liberal paradigm speaks of the bank of flexibility, it is in effect the liberal-democratic city-construction discourse about citizenry that advances the rights of the free pedestrian and car driver against the hawkers. The "general" citizen is described as a classless, innocent neuter whose rights are trimmed by a small group. Thus The Telegraph on 20th April 2007 writes: *civic rights cannot forever remain captive to an illegality that has been allowed to prosper for the convenience of a few.*

The ideal living condition of this citizen is the resort: there where the border between Inside and Outside is clearly defined and a neutral space of quiet and security exists. Directly in the cities of the centre, above the hawkers' stalls, placards of new investor assets are hung in the city space. While the gated communities and resorts at the edge of the global city display a middle-class which acquires neutral space in affluent enclaves and the economy erects IT temples for itself in special zones, the ambivalent intermediate spaces of the centres create the existential basis for millions of marginalised city inhabitants.

A rational discourse about civil rights and public space which does not want to accept the informal economy creates a picture of a city that lets itself be led by thoughts of cleanliness and order. The anti-hawker mood shows the pressure under which Kolkata is to free itself from a negative post-colonial image in the face of global competition, and at the same time to define urbanity and identity for a new middle class. It is not far-fetched to say that the hawkers are excluded from debates about citizenry and how the city of the future should be.

Opinion makers against hawkers stand for a homogenised world view. Neo-liberal city construction tries to smoothen out the differences of everyday life. Parallels between the discourse and the city, between Inside and Outside are evoked: "Our Space, Their Mess" says the Telegraph on 12th April 2006. The title describes the mechanism of a construction of we-spaces about exemption processes. Real connections between middle-class and hawkers are blinded out. Good governance in this context (connected with intolerance towards everything disorderly, incommensurable, unclear) is propagated as an universal remedy, while in reality it leads to a further reduction of complexity of the urban.

The way city planning deals with street peddlers shows how the exclusion procedure is used in the neo-liberal debate about civil rights and public space. An ideology which relies on a historical and conflict-free spaces and also relies on the premise that anyone who follows global market rules has a chance, shows its undercomplexed face. It tries to deny the symbiotic relationship between hawkers and middle-class and thus the complex organisation of urban spaces, and tries to relate to simple we-you patterns instead of a discursive differentiated culture of conflict.

The close meshed networking of city space is not only the living space of the hawkers. The middle-class is closely connected to their space-covering precarious housing situation.

It is the informal sector which provides the "settled" city residents with those essential services which they need for their own reproduction. What separates the middle-class from hawkers is not time or space, but power, economy and partaking in civil rights.

Hawkers are a substantial part of the urban system. Marginalised and criminalised, they are branded as the cause of all urban problems. Municipal administration and the urban elite put the major part of the working city population under the general suspicion of being hindrances to city improvement. Tacit urbanism as the spatial product of a marginalised majority is completely excluded from initiatives for the creation of the city.

One fact persists: no urban planning process can be successful if it is not in the position to accept reality and to integrate the producers of the informal sector.

Tacit urbanism

We must consider how migrants improvise, make do, and create a place for themselves in the city. ~ Ananya Roy.

The urban is neither an a historic phenomenon nor teleologically fixed in terms of linear progression. Different movements combine and superimpose on each other in the differentiations of the urban in time. The urban as a form changes itself constantly and follows no fixed pattern; instead it produces new patterns from urban practice thus space is produced improvisationally. Improvisation means then: constructively working with disorder in a transforming community. The urban unfolds itself in an open process of daily interaction of innumerable subsystems. Disorder creates intensities, absurdities, multiple logic. This disorder lives, informs, surprises and creates higher orders with the passage of time.

One could say that disorder and order constantly interchange in the urban dialectic. It could also be possible to go a step further: the urban calls upon reflections about what order and what disorder actually means in which context, at what time, and in what situation. The urban calls upon reflection and action, and at the same time, Improvisation. This implies the constant development of new patterns of interpretation, called upon to read the urban anew time and again, to discover orders. Because urban practice is cultural appropriation, not obvious but tacit. Tacit urbanism.

Typology

The Living City

Modernism has passed the concept of determined planning, and postmodernism has passed the concept of chaotic fragmentation down to us. Can't there be something in between? A notion of organisation of space in the production itself, as a kind of improvisation technology? That would take into account that living space is constituted by the relations, interactions between connected environmental conditions and actions rather than by isolated forms, buildings.

By looking at this notion of tacit urbanism that unfolds as urban interaction, can't we try to learn from hawking how to make the potential of a situation visible, and project that into a future which enables the urban to perform better?

Hawkers can become a bodily grasping of our understanding of urban reality. This book tries to capture an important part of the living condition of Kolkata, a part that was for a long time not on the map, not in the consciousness of the public, although being prominent in everyday space and life. As we went along, we found that since the National Policy was enacted in 2004, a policy shift is also noticeable in Kolkata. That gives us hope for the future of the living city.

Typology

It is surprising how dense the street life of Kolkata actually is. The informal sector economy forms the background for the diverse spatial compositions and functional combinations of the hawker sidewalk economy. What is it about the urban form of Kolkata that allows such imaginative productions?

In such a specific situation, architectural design doesn't hold that much of an interest. It is the turning of urban space into a resource, which makes the Kolkata pavements so particular. As architects it is far more interesting on how to take advantage of such practice than to turn away from it. That may start with a change of perspective and to put the hawkers' practice on the map. It also includes interpreting hawking not only as an economic device, but also as cultural practice contributing to the interaction of daily life. It is an asset that provides goods directly to the doorsteps, and so keeps residents from driving to far away shopping malls, congesting the city even more. Hawking is not chaos but rather an expression of the concrete urban situation of everyday Kolkata.

In our survey we have selected portraits of hawker stands. They are divided into typologies derived from specific functions and uses: food vending, hairdressing or the time of non-use. Although these types are not taken into account in urban planning, they explain to a large extent what Kolkata is. The types are, out of economic reasons, constructed in a very pragmatic manner using the possible elements of that space or situation. The highly economical efficiency is guided by the rule of minimum effort and maximal mobility. At the same time they are not just physical spaces, they are also connected to the cultural level of the space. Hawkers use whatever is at hand. By taking advantage of already existing elements: electric wiring, municipal street signs, walls of residential buildings, footpath ground, they re-use and re-interpret spatial by-products. The material available also has to be used in an innovative manner. Hawking as spatial practice thus establishes a second layer, a second role to build environment. An urban ecology of use unfolds. The footpath and the buildings perform several roles within the multiple urban situations.

By treating the relation of the elements as the major issue, we try to see the problem as openly as we can. We looked at the issue flatly, getting information from different sides: the hawker, the hawker union, the police, the architect, the municipal corporation and the NGO. This way we show that the physical composition of space is very much connected to the political issue of organizing urban space.

In this respect, urban space cannot be described as chaotic or confused, nor predetermined, but as a constant process in the making.

Interview Transcripts

01 Hawker Sangram Committee

I am Anadi Saha. I work for the Calcutta Hawkermens' Union since 1980. I am also a hawker.

The HSC includes 42 different hawkers' unions.

In 1997 the West Bengal government Transport Department said, that from January 1997 onwards they would not allow hawkers to be on the streets because they were causing disruptions in the traffic.

Calcutta Hawkermens' Union was the main union of the hawkers. And they came together with other unions and discussed organising in 1995. The HSC still hadn't been formed. On the 9th of August 1996 the HSC was formed. It became a sort of an umbrella organisation for the 42 unions in Kolkata. The HSC decided that no hawker could be removed from the streets because 60 to 70% of the people depended on this for their livelihood. On selling, on buying, whatever it is.

One month before "Operation Sunshine" started, we kept vigil every night, because we knew that these raids were going to take place, to remove us from the streets. 4000 policemen and paramilitary, 8 deputy commissioners of the Police, the party cadres, all were armed and ready. And they did this whole thing over night. Strangely enough, 23rd of November 1996 it was reported in the newspapers that the Transport Minister Subhash Chakraborty, who is still the Transport Minister, told the newspaper that no problem, we have talked to the unions, the hawkers have agreed and they will very peacefully evacuate and let us do our thing. But actually that was not true. For one month we had been keeping vigil, we stayed up all night and made sure the shops were on the pavements. So when the news came that all would take place peacefully, we decided to go home and rest a bit. And on the 23rd midnight the police came in with full force from Shyambazar, north Kolkata and Gariahat, more or less all at the same time. It was a very big operation for the government. We tried to resist, but who are we? We are only hawkers. They were armed.

Although we resisted, there was also trust. Because hawkers are mostly from lower or middle class backgrounds. We could not believe that the Communist Party that was in the government, the same party we supported, who we believed were for us, would turn against us. That was also a reason why the forces could do this thing so suddenly over night; they took us by surprise.

Hawkers are not antisocial people. We are not hooligans. We are people who are working at the lower levels of economy, at the grassroots. Historically there have always been hawkers. 500, 600 years ago, there were also hawkers. They walked with things on their heads and shoulders from house to house selling goods, or maybe they sat at the street corner and sold something for some time.

These were the arguments that we put up not only before the government, but also the intelligentsia. To let them know, that we are not antisocial and we have no opportunities to get jobs so we are forced to do this kind of business. So the first thing of our strategy was to put an argument forward.

The second argument that we were putting forth to the public and the government was that we are there to supply goods to people with lower economic means. Not only that, we are able to deliver goods to a person's doorstep at a cheaper rate. And we tried to tell the bigger companies, look that's what we can do for you. The bigger shops, the shopping malls are not going to give this service. Also we have an informal bazar among ourselves where we do a lot of buying and sourcing of our goods. It is a network, that allows us to keep prices low and provide home delivery of a large variety of goods.

The third argument was: the food diversity and quality. We offer 300 different varieties of food for 5 rupees or less. And the All India Institute of Hygiene and Public Health actually did a study and found that nowhere else in this country, or in the world, is such a variety available at such a low cost. Food that has good quality, nutritional benefits for the normal person. 1000 calories between 5 to 7 rupees is provided to anybody who buys this food.

The media have supported us partially, sometime they have been against us. But our strongest argument still is, that without us, a lot of people from the lower income range will not be supplied with goods. It would not just be a handful of hawkers who would be affected, but a huge circle depends on us as their marketing agency, as their outlet to sell the home-based productions. These are all small-scale productions, in the districts, the villages.

For the last 3 years we have chosen 4 places that are model places, Prototypes on how to formalise our practice and control quality. These are Park Street, Chowringhee Road, and other close by places. We have taught the hawkers at those places: one, you have to occupy only one third of the pavement, so that the public, the pedestrians can move and not affect the traffic.

300 members were trained by the All India Institute of Hygiene and Public Health on how to prepare food on the road, how to buy, how to keep things clean. And those 300 people went and trained others to do the same thing. They are not allowed plastic, they have umbrellas, the vegetables must be fresh everyday, food should not be heated less than 36 degrees Celsius, the garbage should be kept at one particular spot so it can be easily cleaned. So we have started taking these steps. And since this started 3 years ago, the Bengal Health Minister Surjya Kanti Misra, and the United Nations

and various other bodies came and did a check. They realized that as far as street food is concerned, this was the correct way to do it.

So the union expanded from the economic and political function to the educational function.

There are approximately 275,000 hawkers in Kolkata right now of which 10% are organized by the Communist Party trade union (CITU) and the rest of them are with the HSC. That means that every hawker is organized although his trade is categorized as the unorganized sector.

The main office is the HSC. But the other 42 unions also have their own organizers. We communicate with them and they pass it down to their members. That's how we communicate. There are some unions which are spread all over the city but there are also some which are localized. Like at Gariahat Crossing, the Indira Hawkers Union is only responsible for that area.

{Mr Murad Hussain, Working President of HSC adds: I am going out to the districts to make sure that all the communication is passed down correctly and if there are any clarifications to be made, I do it on behalf of the HSC. Every union has different committees that have meetings at various levels}.

On 4th February 2008 we are having a meeting of all hawkers unions in India. There are 40,00,000 hawkers in this country. So the government of India has enacted a National Policy for Street Vendors in India.

The National Policy now has to be implemented by all state governments. So, in Kolkata, the Municipal Corporation (KMC) has set up an Apex Committee which is looking into these things. But it has been made clear: no hawkers can be removed from anywhere, provided they stay within the guidelines: only one third of the pavement, no plastics, no permanent structures, no blocking the carriage way and street corners, stay away within the radius of 50 feet from the centre of important crossings.

In the future there will be other things, which is supply of water, health and sanitary facilities, to be provided by the KMC.

The Mayor of Kolkata is the Chairman of the Apex Committee, which has the Police Commissioner, three mayors in council, and the rest are members of the HSC.

But it is possible that we will see another big eviction drive. Because the political party that we supported at one time, the Communists, are now attracting the multimillionaires, the global players to come to the State.

But we will resist. There is a national policy and we have a national federation which is the main body of the hawkers in India. So as a body we are going to resist in Delhi. And here we will fight too, it's a battle, a struggle.

We have been very proactive in our fight for our civic rights. We know that there are problems. At the same time, we have decided that while we are continuing the struggle, we are talking to the government about social benefits for the hawkers like medical insurance, some sort of pension, because after working for 40, 50 years the hawkers go back with nothing except disease. So we have tied up various institutes in the country. One suggestion is that the government pays three rupees and the hawker will pay one rupee per month to set up a fund for these hawkers.

There is a bill, which will be placed in the coming parliament session at Delhi on the unorganised sector of India and the hawkers have also been included in this sector. In that way we hope that the legalization process continues. The step from the unorganised, informal, perhaps illegal sector to the legal sector is happening in stages. We feel that there is some progress.

If the local government tries to evict us and go against the National Policy then the name HSC will show its meaning: Sangram in Bengali means struggle. So we will jointly resist as a people's movement.

One of the reasons we have been able to progress is because in India there is a large anti-globalisation movement. Because we are small independent sellers of cheap reasonable goods, the people support us.

On the 8th of January 1997, John Major, then the Prime Minister of Great Britain was supposed to come with various businessmen and industrialists for a conference to Kolkata. It was organised by the CII, Confederation of Indian Industry. We had the feeling that the whole change in policy against the hawkers was because of these industrialists and businessmen. So we feel the pressure of globalisation. On 8th January all the hawkers of Kolkata came out in a massive protest rally. This caused John Major to postpone his trip and to arrive on the next day. We were very successful, because we also got the support of the common people, the intelligentsia and others who are also against gobalisation.

The HSC has also started a new thing:

In the food sector, for example, we pack products ourselves, like oil, and distribute it to the hawkers to raise the quality.

In the garment sector, a quality control unit has been started to check the quality of the products being sold on the street.

The committee raises money from subscriptions. Members of the Hawkermens Union pay 2 rupees per day. The other unions pay 10 rupees per month per member, but this often doesn't happen.

Besides that we have founded a school for street children and we run a public toilet outside this building to raise money. 10 full time members are employed here. We cook food ourselves. To organize the city we don't need maps, we have the space memory in our heads.

The 26th of May is International Hawkers Day.

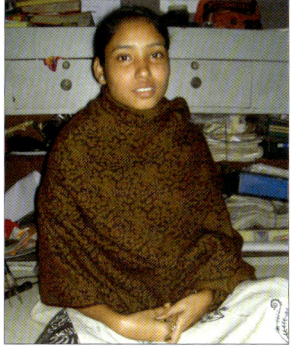

02 Hawker Sangram Committee

My name is Anita Das.

More and more women have begun to join the union, because many of the men in the family are not well off, they don't have jobs. So I am looking after the women's part of the HSC in West Bengal.

The women earn the same money as men do.

As vegetable vendors, they themselves go to the market to buy fresh produce, bring them to the city and sell it. They are independent, so we communicate directly with them.

In the Hawkermen's Union the women comprise 55%. There are some areas designated only for women hawkers. For example, the Howrah and Sealdah railway stations.*

We have a system. Nobody can just come there and sit down. Just as you have admission to a school. When you want to sit somewhere you have to go through our organisation and ask for permission.

Every area has a leader. If you want to sell in a particular area you first have to approach that leader. He brings it up to our committee and then we make a decision: yes or no.

Sometimes there are vendors who are not part of the union. If they get into trouble with the police, they often come to us, become a member and then the union takes care of their case.

The members of the Hawkermen's Union do not have to pay "hafta" to the police.

_____

* We jest with Anadi Saha, interviewed earlier, that the Calcutta Hawkermen's Union should consider a name change under such circumstances. He smiles shyly and says, "no, it's a lucky name for us." Anita too, smiles and nods.

The women wake up at three or four o'clock in the morning and go to the bazar to buy the things. The children are usually taken care of by the mother-in-law or the grandparents, the husband, or whoever is at home. Anyway, people who come from such a poor background learn to take care of themselves at a very young age.

The women come into the city by the first train and go back to the village on the last train in the evening. 90% of the vendors come from outside the city. They need around three or four hours to go back and forth. They travel by local train because they have a lot of goods to carry. So coming in a bus is not convenient. At certain times trains are very crowded.

The population density of Kolkata during the day and during the night is very different.

Seven years ago I started by working for the school for street children, which is led by HSC. While I was here with Shaktiman Ghosh, I started taking part in the meetings and showing interest, that is how I slowly moved into this part of the situation.

It is my dream that women hawkers become more and more involved in this whole movement. They should not restrict themselves to just being vendors of goods. There are already women who take part in the meetings, give speeches, but I want more of them. I want women to become more and more active in uplifting themselves through their own dreams.

More and more time has to be spent with the women, organising them, talking to them, discussing things with them, finding out their problems, trying to find out ways to take care of it. For example, from the union side, one of the biggest problems is for women to be able to conveniently use the toilet. So we tell the leaders to ask the women about their needs and we try to take care of it. I know it will take a long time. But I am positive that it will happen.

03 Hawker Sangram Committee

I am Sudipto Moitra, a functionary of the HSC.

Actually the local government is implementing the national policy to regulate the hawkers within the city frame. In this situation regulation is not happening everywhere in the same way. Somewhere it works, somewhere it doesn't. Because it is just one year that this started. So the media sometimes reports that these places are not well regulated. In this case they feel insecure if people take photos, because they think they are media people and will show our situation on TV, which is maybe not favouring the hawkers.

At Sealdah many people move in and out. It is the main connection for the suburbs. So this is an important place, because the people, when they have finished their work, come to the station and buy vegetables from the hawkers for their homes.

That is a place for women vendors. We have done a survey on them. Their life is very hectic. They wake up in the mornings between 3:30 and 4, then they have to cook for their family, go to the local market and buy vegetables from the farmers. They come to Sealdah to sell their goods from 7 in the morning and have to stay there the whole day because the vegetable are also sold in the evening. Then they return home at night, 10 or10:30. In that area, they have a problem as there is no proper urinal for the women. Because of that some of the women have medical problems.

From the very beginning we have stood up for the argument that if the hawker could be regulated, we can make a legal framework for them.

In the model hawker zones the union has employed two to three persons to clean the pavements three times a day. So unions can also take responsibility for cleanliness. Hawker and pedestrians, HSC and KMC can coexist.

You have different legal spaces in the city. At the Sealdah station the law is under the railway authority. So the KMC has to talk to the railways for that particular space. After finalising the hawkers policy they have to sort out particular cases. Some other spaces in the city are under the Metro railway authority and others the military. In these areas the KMC cannot enforce their policies. That's why sometimes many authorities are involved in the regulation process.

Even if we regulate, we are still not legal. But the National Policy at least forces the local government to accept the hawkers.

In Article 6 the National Policy states that section 283 of the Indian Penal Code and section 34 of the police act concerning obstruction of public way or place, are deterrents to street vending. They cause a contradiction between a 'legal' licensed vendor and 'illegal' obstruction. In Article 6.2 therefore, the policy recommends that the central Government and all States should amend the Police Act and Rules/Regulations thereunder and add a rider as follows: "Except in case of street vendors/ hawkers and service providers with certain reasonable regulations." So that the conflict with the law could be avoided.

But this is only a guideline. If the local government wants to, it can avoid or skip this.

That's why we have to build a proper movement to put pressure on the authorities.

We have done a national campaign in different states, as well as agitations and rallies. Then, after a lot of negotiation on different levels, the national government formed a task force on vendors. Our chairman Shaktiman Ghosh was also part of this task force.

You see, there was no Policy before 2004. After that Policy was passed, for one year there was no implementation process in India. So after that we had to start again to build up pressure. And now there are many places where the Policy is implemented. But it needs the unions.

The Apex Committee is the main body in Kolkata to work out local policies. The Apex meets once a month. In the first meeting of the Apex on the 7th of June 2006, four main regulations were laid out.

One of the biggest problems hawkers are facing now is globalisation. Big companies like Wal-Mart and Metro, as also many domestic companies like Tata, Reliance, Spencers, are also entering the retail market now with vegetables, food and goods. They are opening shops all over India and they are tough competition for the hawkers. Because they are giving packages of pizza and Coke for 6 to 12 rupees. The corporate Indian retail market is the greatest threat to hawkers. And all over India the battle begins. The hawkers started the protest and in some regions they have even become violent, destroying some shops. Reliance buys goods directly from the farmers, sometimes they are doing contract farming. They are coming up with vegetables at a very cheap rate. They have their own cold storage where they can store food for years. We are going through a very big transition period in India. The corporate domination over people is being enforced at a fast rate. The rights, the resources, the people's lands, all are going to corporate houses. It is the free market policy started in India in the 90s. Spencers has already opened 5 retail markets in Kolkata in a period of one year. And Wal-Mart too has entered India.

04 Hawker, Esplanade

My name is Said Hussein.

I have worked here for 40 years. I started when I was 12 years old. From the age of 12 I've been doing this. I found no other way to earn money.

The shop itself is owned by somebody else. I work for that person.

I have worked for the same man for 40 years. A brother of mine knew this man, and through him I got to know this person. And that's how I started.

I'm originally from Bihar. But I came to Kolkata because here I have the opportunity to earn money.

I came to Kolkata around 1965,1966. The family mostly stays in Bihar. They keep coming and going. Most of the time they stay there and I stay here. I lost my father when I was very young. So there was no option for me. I could not think of missing the family, I had to earn some money to send it to my mother, my sister, my brother. I feel good about the fact that I can help them. But it has not got something to do with being proud. It's a very realistic thing, I have to earn the money anyway.

I start at 10 in the morning. I live close by, so it takes me about 20 minutes to walk here.

I get my products across the river beyond the Howrah station, from another place called Mourigram. I have to go there to get the things.

Nobody else can come to this place. It's only for this shop, my shop.

Sometimes when the big bosses get a little tough we have to remove the stall for one or two days. But most of the time it's a permanent place. I don't have to pay any "hafta".

I am a member of the Hawker Sangram Committee for more than ten years now. Earlier I was with the Forward Bloc, which is a political party. I changed to HSC, because it is not political. When we were with the party, those people were not able to give us the support to remain here, because they are also a constituent of the leftist government of Bengal. Whereas Shaktiman Ghosh of the HSC he gave us support, and he made sure that we were able to stay here.

I earn 120 rupees a day. But if I sell more, I can make more money. I get a commission of 10% of the sales that I make.

I have no other option, I have to be happy.

05 Hawker , Gariahat Crossing

My name is Amar Das.

I'm from Kasba. That's down the road, twenty minutes from here. In the morning I arrive here at 10 o'clock and I return at 9 in the evening. I have been here since 1978.

Since 1972 there have been stalls here on the street. In 1977, when the Left Front government came to power, they kind of unofficially made us legal. We were allowed to stay here. But in 1996 they removed us from here. All the stalls were broken down. The whole place, when all that happened with Operation Sunshine. At that that time I was roaming around with bags. And then again the laws were relaxed. I came and occupied this space. And after that I have been here with an unofficial sanction. It is not a legal sanction. We have struggled, we have negotiated, we have fought with the government as a group, as a body of hawkers. We have fought to be able to occupy this space. And currently the present Chief Minister Buddhadev Bhattacharya seems to be in favour of us. He is not making too much effort to remove us from here. And we also try to keep to the rules. We can only occupy one third of the pavement. So we try to do that, the rest of the pavement is for pedestrians.

I get some of my products from Burrabazar, the wholesale market. That's mostly stuff that comes from Bombay, Delhi and other cities. But most of the products that I have is made by small cottage industries in the districts of Bengal. And those people, the manufacturers themselves come to me and give it to me. It is not only us, who are fighting for survival, it is also those people. Not only the people that are manufacturing, also the ones who make the fabric. They are all artisans from the rural area. Tiny industries. The reason why we are able to sell for cheap prices is because most of the things are made by the women in the family, who after they do their housework, take their sewing-machines and they make two or three bags or whatever they can. They sell it for less, so I'm able to sell it for less. Whereas when I buy stuff from the wholesale market, I have to sell it for a higher price. It is coming through many middlemen who keep their commissions.

The people from the rural area now come directly as they now know me personally. But otherwise, if they come to this area, they know that there are many shops who will buy from them. Not just Gariahat, they can also go to New Market, Esplanade or north Calcutta

West Bengal, historically, is a place where employment isn't easy to get. So in 1978, I was a worker here, in one of these stalls. When that stall was broken down, I had nowhere to go and no money. Then I somehow raised some money, bought some things and roamed the streets, with the things in my hands and sold them.

I like my work a lot. Besides making money, I can meet other people, have a friendly chat with everybody. But I wish that it would be a more secure, a more organised work, with better infrastructure. The construction of my stall is not very good, my products are not really protected. So a few days ago when it rained, there was no business at all, I could not set up my shop. Two days without business means a lot of money down the drain.

06. Hawker, Gariahat Crossing

My Name is Pappu Das.

I come here in the morning at 10 o'clock. I live in Kasba. It's not very far the road down from here. I get here on the autos.

Everyday I bring my stuff, lay it out here and then I take it back again in the evening. Because of low economic standard and financial problems in the family I decided to do something where I really work hard and try to make a living.

I get my products from Burrabazar, the wholesale market. It is located in north Kolkata. For some things I go there and buy, for other things guys come and deliver to me. Everytime they come, I place the order for the next time.

I have tied up all my products, so when the police comes I'm ready to run. Otherwise this is my space. Earlier, there were stalls here. But when Operation Sunshine came, everything was demolished. Then this place became empty, and me and my partner occupied this space. And then we had to negotiate with the Indira Hawkers Union and they permitted us to occupy this space. There is no union-office as such. But there are some of these "big" guys, some of the leaders, some of them have stalls here and we just negotiate on the footpath itself. They have a registered office, where they have bigger meetings or other functions. But thats not where we have to go.

I like the work, I make money out of it. But the guys with the stalls, they have a system. They have been given a certain amount of space where there is three square feet or whatever and they can sit there all day and sell things without a problem. No policeman will come and bother them. But us, who operate in this space here, we have to run away every time the police comes. So we have an insecure time. Sometimes we have a good sale and the police comes. Then we run and lose our sales. We hope that some time we are given a space of our own which we can occupy without the police bothering us. We want the right to stay. Right now we operate within the forbidden zone: 50 feet radius from the center of the crossing.

Typology: Food, Restaurants

Typology: Food, Restaurants

Typology: Food, Restaurants

Interview Transcripts

07 Mr Hari Rajan, Additional Commissioner, Kolkata Police

Public space as in India you see in Germany only on Octoberfest. Otherwise it is very calm.

The Apex Committee is chaired by the Mayor, the people of the HSC are there and myself as the Additional Commissioner of Police. The government is not directly represented in the APEX meeting. We are compassionate towards the hawkers, by taking into account his livelihood. And at the same time to take care that there is no inconvenience caused for the other road users.

Now you have Town Planners that say that hawking zones should be given, but earlier the hawker was not part of the scheme of things. At the same time the other road users, mainly the pedestrians are not able to use the footpath which it is primarily meant for. The third point is: in residential areas, hawkers have become a nuisance because only the person who stays there knows them. So the residents won't complain, but the other road users will. It is a very difficult balancing task. And if anybody gets on to the intersections the people cannot move from one side of the road to the other. Crossings are supposed to be kept free. This is what we are trying to do. And the Apex Committee lays down the broad principles taking into view the interests of all.

By the mid-90s a change of consciousness came. With the employment rate watering down and the landholding shrinking, people migrated to urban areas and there was a strain on the footpath and the carriageway, the water supply, because a lot of them live on the road itself. They live on the place they occupy. Many cannot afford residential space. The problem would be less, if they cook elsewhere, buy their merchandise to come and sell on the streets and go back.

They come from the suburbs or the villages, so to return everyday is not very convenient and very expensive, so they stay there. Maybe the family stays elsewhere, but the breadwinner and also sometime his spouse stay at their hawking place. And once a week they probably go home.

Our city is old, very traditional, no broad roads, not very broad footpaths. Only 6% of road space, and you don't have any restriction on registration of cars, vehicles and what-have-you. That is why it is a very fine balancing act. If you think only of the hawkers, you can't think of the other road users and vice versa.

It is very difficult to enforce a change on a daily basis unless there is a self-regulation. Only one third of the footpath can be used by the hawker. Now who is going to police this? The unions have to regulate their members. For the Police to do this, you need a massive establishment, like a special hawker police. Because a local police station and the traffic police cannot cope with policing these things. So there needs to be a lot of cooperation.

It is right, in 1996 there was the massive raid Operation Sunshine. But again we couldn't hold on to their places. It is extremely difficult given the economic scenario. People have to live. So they slowly came back.

In hundred major intersections 50 feet has to be kept clear. We can't keep the doors open for everybody to hawk. Because sometimes even my courtyard can turn into a hawking ground. Every public space, including parks will turn into hawking grounds. So we have to say: thus far and no further. Because the city has its own physical limitations. If we were spread in a very linear fashion, in a very planned manner, then you can expect, as the population increases, as livelihood chances have to be better, we can make them sit. But they all converge to the central business district. So what will happen to the others? The pedestrians, car drivers etc. They also have a livelihood. The man in the office, he has to come on time. So we have to harmonize multiple interests.

No one wants to become a hawker. No child will say I want to become a hawker in my life. So that is an economic issue. People study hawkers, they do docu-features on hawkers but nobody wants to become a hawker. You only become a hawker because of a lack of better alternatives.

After the first green revolution the second green revolution is yet to come. The fertility of land is lower, the cost of production higher. Use of fertilizers has caused incidence of cancer in people in Punjab. We hit a limit as far as food production is concerned. And if you can't keep the population in check you have to go to the service sector. People without education work in the traditional old service sectors like hawking, food stalls etc.

We communicate trough the Transport Department because they are obviously concerned with traffic. But also to our own Administrative Department.

The political leaders think about these problems. Because every five years they have to go back to the electorate. They are not bureaucrats who stay on for 40 years, get into the service once and then slowly be promoted. They have to do a promotion test every 5 years. And that is not so easy. It is very easy for me to criticize sitting here on a permanent chair, virtually. But is is extremely difficult for him to do the balancing act.

Last 40 years, the police was really in a bad shape. But now we are getting a lot of money. From the government of India we have a program called Vision 2010. So from 2000 to 2010 the government will spend 2200 crores on modernizing the police. 30% has to be contributed by the state government and 70% will be contributed by the central government. A lot of projects they approve, which we couldn't think of earlier. Arms, equipment, communication, transport, buildings. But not salaries.

But that doesn't necessarily lead to corruption, bribing. That happens even in Italy, where the people are paid very well. I read an article that the Minister in Italy dismissed a huge number of officers. He was quoted in the Internet: "I don't want them to jump on motorists from behind bushes." So some of it is there. But I wouldn't guarantee that if you have very good salaries, that bribery will vanish. Because given the materialistic way of life today, everyone wants to own a LCD or a plasma or a colour TV etc.

Or a Nano. But that is a different thing. Because necessarily we have to subsidise urban transport. All across the world urban transport was always subsidised.

Now it is a different question whether you run it efficiently so the subsidy will be less. That leads to the high occupancy of vehicles being on the road thereby encouraging personalized transport. The moment one finds traveling by public transport painful, one will even pledge their house or wife's jewellery to buy a two-wheeler. If it is a little bit more affordable, why not a Nano? Ultimately it has to peak somewhere, then they again have to come in for a Metro or something. Because once you have thousands of cars on the road, then the delay becomes very painful. Then the society has to think about traveling on Mars.

Public transport I firmly believe is the only solution. Personalized transport will always catch up with any infrastructure that is being set up. You see the flyovers, now you have jams at each end. What are you going to do? We have to think of an elevated corridor? That will get saturated too. We have to think about whether to subsidise public transport by saving on flyovers, or to encourage personalised transport and build more flyovers. This is a policy decision that has to be taken by the government.

As a bureaucrat you have certain limitations of advising the government. Because one, you are not a qualified transportation engineer. Two, it is more the academicians who can influence. I have only ground-level experience. So I can go only so far.

Yes we do communicate, we do exchange our minds, but whether it gets enacted in policy is a little difficult.

For instance the auto-rickshaws. Auto-rickshaws are contract carriages, but they become stage carriages. A contract carriage is a metered vehicle which will take you anywhere from point A to point B and the contract is only between one person and the vehicle owner and the driver. The stage carriages pick up and set down passengers at predetermined stops and also has a fare-chart which is approved by the local transport authority. Now auto-rickshaws who are contract vehicles have been converted, not only in Kolkata, into stage carriages. So again the economics changes. I'd rather pay ten rupees and go in an auto-rickshaw than pay 5 rupees and go in a bus. So there is a market distortion that takes place where the investment in buses gets reduced and the investment in auto-rickshaws increases. This is the second set of problems after personalised transport. Where it becomes part personalised, part public transport. First personalized as long as you travel, but otherwise it's a public transport.

The reason behind this is that high occupancy public transport has not been encouraged or subsidised. And again there is an employment angle to this. Because a bus employs two to three people and one auto-rickshaw employs one person. And it can take the place of ten to twelve buses. But a bus can carry 50 to 60 passengers and auto-rickshaw is supposed to carry not more than 3. So 60 by three is twenty. Twenty auto-rickshaws can create chaos on a road. Even if you expect a bus to be driven by someone like Bruce Willis or Keanu Reeves, auto-rickshaws can create real chaos. They can just turn around, go in circles and stall the entire corridor. The sum of the parts are more than the whole: twenty auto-rikshas can create more chaos than by a bus driven by someone who is totally drunk.

In many other cities the shared auto-system has come. There is a new Piaggio, a ten seater. This again will create enough trouble vis-a-vis a bus. We are talking about the bus rapid transport system, BRTS. A kilometre can cost you about 10 to 12 crores. That is one of the best and most intelligent transport systems. With prioritised signalling, advance communication to the passengers. 10 to 12 crores against a Metro which will cost you about 200 crores. Can we afford it? 168 are the official costs, but there are hidden costs like custom concessions, duty concessions? The other way to look at it is: can we use fertile land to build roads? Or should we go under ground and spend that money?

Take the 12 crores and with the rest of the money, 178 crores, subsidise the farmer. I'm just thinking aloud. This is not official policy. But I have taken particular interest because I was DC Traffic here in 2001. I do read literature, which is available on the net. So we have to decide what we are going to do?

We can't ape the west because we have a mass population. And our landholdings are small. Our densities are very very large. We have to think in our own way. Does one need a chaffeur-driven car or can one come to the office by train? We need an informed public opinion. Unfortunately simple ordering of things is not possible. At Delhi we have a large think tank that reflects on BRTS. That's why Delhi, Bangalore, Hyderabad and other cities are all going for BRTS. But all for new areas, new alignments, new roads - this can be done. With existing roads, how much can we do? We have to work out a cost-benefit analysis of something like a big dig project like Boston where they keep the surface clean as a public park and allow transport to run underneath the road; whether that'll cost less than running a train service underground. Or do we allow all kinds of transport to take the tunnel.

First thing is conservation of power. Then traffic solutions, that includes parking. The third would also be security. When we do town planning, we should plan in such a way, that blocks can be cut off during the nights with just one checkpost or a dropgate. So the entire block can sleep peacefully. I'm talking of Salt Lake and other new townships. First should be intelligent buildings which conserve power. Because we can all go down in floods due to global warming. Then we have traffic circulation which again is connected with fuel conservation and greenhouse gases. And the third is urban security. Urban security should be a component of urban planning. Because I can't place policemen all around that block.

I wish we transform our city into a modern one with a traditional touch. That means neighbours should be talking to each other everyday, neighbourhoods should be interacting with each other. In the multistoried buildings we don't know the neighbour. That's why you find servants killing the owners and slipping away. We have to keep the traditional part as far as practicable. And modernise so that it is clean, the air is clean. What else can I wish? Prosperity, lots of employment and control on the population. You can't impose this of course, that is also a matter of self-regulation. But that has changed already.

I used to know a constable who had 6 children. Now most of my policemen have one child. There is a new awareness, at least among the policemen. A constable 20 years ago was making 3000 rupees. Having 6 children, bribery for him is something which is a godsend. And also because of the bribery he maybe isn't even concerned about having so many children. He thinks that god will take care of him. This is a Hindu rate of growth in a different sense. So when god allows me to procreate it is his act not mine. And he will also find the food for it. So many say, what can I do? It is god's will, I will have my seventh child. Now this has changed. They all know: small family is better. We can live within a budget, we don't have to tend towards credit nor bribery.

So we have to think of a new way. Compare it with China. China has a massive land mass, we don't. West Bengal has a population density of around 990 persons per square kilometer. It is the highest in the country. So to move people out for any sort of development, means you are not transplanting them but you are just evicting them. Unfortunately none of the papers carry this facet of it. We have about 26% forest. If you exclude the forest areas it will go up to 1200 persons per square kilometer. Against Tamilnadu's 385. I found it is very high if you leave the forest out, which is not available directly to the citizen. Nobody talks about that. You can't sustain a population like that on land. But how much of available land can we afford to lose? We need food. In the west population is low and resources widespread. In the east it is exactly the opposite. In Germany you might have sausages everyday. I have it once a month.

- gets phone call -

For example this bookstore in the Shreeram Arcade shopping centre. That fellow called us up to help him. So we evicted all the hawkers there after the Apex started meeting. Now they all came back, shouting all the more. What can you do? The HSC agreed upon clearing 58 crossings, but I have a list of 200. So it is a constant negotiation.

08 Officer In Charge, Gariahat Police Station

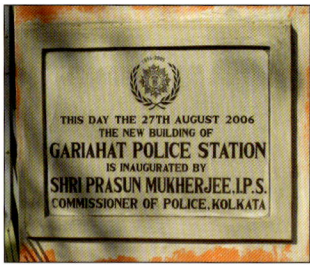

Gariahat is in a process. We have the problem that the hawkers occupy most of the pavement. So pedestrians have to walk on the streets. That causes chaos, accidents. The police is always regarded as being responsible. The pavement and roads are the property of the KMC. So we have to keep them safe.

Everyday we look after the crossing. We get information about problems, so we react. Sometimes by landlords, sometimes by shop owners. But once the hawkers are away, the shop owners do the same thing: put all their stuff on the pavement.

There is the hawker drive. The Calcutta local act provides us with a law with which we can prosecute the hawkers. When they are arrested, they can take bail and pay a fine of 15 to 20 rupees. But before we prosecute we warn them. We talk to the union leaders and tell them if anyone is not behaving right. We always contact the HSC.

Some of the hawkers are there, illegally for 30, 40 years. We cannot just tell them to go away, it's their working place. So we are trying to streamline them. The hawkers have nothing else to maintain their families.

We are facing two problems: traffic, and law and order problems. Because if there is an accident, and we don't arrive, the people will burn the car which caused the accident right there on the street.

Population density and population growth are the main problems. In Kolkata it is technically not possible to extend the roads and pavements.

Gariahat is a transit place. 400,000 to 500,000 people come daily to

Gariahat crossing everyday. Gariahat is probably the main junction in south Kolkata. You can go from here to all the places. They come from all over. In the outskirts you know if you want to go to Kolkata, you can go via Gariahat.

Normally 20 cars can pass in one second. But in this crowded situation, 20 cars can only pass in 10 seconds. Cars stand in line at the crossing.

We have too many cars. And with the Tata Nano it's going to be worse. There is no space, not for driving, not for parking. Sometimes cars are being stolen just to get a parking place.

Space is too expensive. In this area you pay 4000 rupees per square metre residential space and 20,000 rupees per square metre for commercial space. No hawker can afford that. The capita income of the average person in Kolkata is 7000 per annum. That's why the problem is there.

In this society there are so many problems.

Typology: Clothing, Laundry

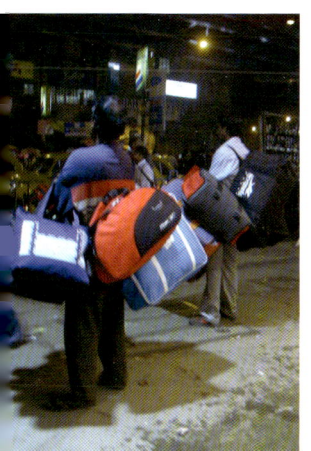

Interview Transcripts

09 Senior Officer, Solid Waste Management
Kolkata Municipal Corporation

This is the KMC Hawker Policy. After you read this, there will be no more questions.

But too many things have yet to be implemented.

The Apex has identified 58 crossings which are very important where no hawkers are allowed within a radius of 50 feet from the center. But there are more crossings that have to be finalised.

We are not evicting hawkers. The Policy regulates hawking and that too for specific areas. So a hawker can sit. That is clear. All the rules are there. In the policy you will see that we have identified areas where they cannot sit, like main gates of schools, residential areas, government offices. The policy has been formulated, now it depends on the HSC and hawkers themselves if they obey these rules. But still 90% of the hawkers they are not following this. That is the problem. Yes the union leaders they are cooperating with the corporation, police and everything but for the ground level people the message is not communicated nicely. They know these things but they also know that maybe once in a month the KMC will come to regulate it. So one day in a month and the rest 29 days they can do their business the way they want. That is the problem. Willingness of all the hawkers, not only the HSC, KMC and police is important.

Yes we are trying to inform, to educate. We are campaigning, and we are also doing not eviction, but some special drives. So if they violate the rules, these are the dates on which we arrange the drive with the help of Kolkata Police. In fact today there is a drive. This,

you can say is an awareness campaign. Because when we are going we are just looking to see if they are following the rules. If not, we tell them. If they are using plastic or permanent structures, if it is there we seize it.

I can show you on my mobile how we are conducting this, not eviction, but regulation drive: today I received a message, I read it to you: the HET (Hawker Eviction Team), this is an old name, CD, central division of Maidan Police Station to be send on 11/02/08 may instead be detailed on 13th, because 11th is a holiday. That was a mistake, the earlier message indicated that on the 11th there will be the drive. But now it says that instead of the 11th it will be on the 13th. In view of Saraswati Puja. So we will send our team and jointly we will regulate this.

In earlier times hawker were not allowed to sit at all. Now it is regulated.

The Hawker Unions are very cooperative but you know, these things are not very costly: one tin sheet, one bench so this is it. Now they arrange again and sit. That is the problem. That is the problem to formalise the informal.

But this is a new policy so let us see. If the hawker will not follow this, our mayor will take some tough decisions. You see, some part of the policy is old. We didn't put a date on it because we made it for a visit of the Delhi Corporation, we handed this over to them. But here you see, there is a new part. It says: "During the process of implementation of hawker policy several questions/points were raised from different corners and the members of the apex committee accordingly revisited the whole thing and has taken following decisions." Then you see several points. At point 12 it says: "Implementation of hawker policy already taken by apex committee is the responsibility of all the hawker unions. KMC and police authority will take appropriate course of action where the unions will fail to implement the policy." And in point 1 you see: "No hawker will be allowed within 50 feet of the 58 important road crossings. In case of any violation hawker concerned will be arrested."

So depending on the situation we are changing our policy. One part is the policy we have prepared jointly one year back, but now we are imposing some new policies. That is all decided by the apex.

What we are saying is: you follow theses rules, you implement the policy then we will discuss other issues like better infrastructure, whether we will give you permission, license, identity card. So this is the first step in the process. So the whole process hasn't yet been legalised, up to now it is just self-regulation. First we have to tackle the organisational level, then we get to the infrastructural level.

It is not the problem of 40000 or 60000 people. But I am no politician, I cannot say anything. The Hawker can only use the space that is existing, but beyond that ....

It is not only a population or a traffic problem, it is also a waste management problem. The hawkers do their business throw away their waste all day. Who can maintain the footpath like that, unless they do it on their own? That is why last time we told the HSC: it is your responsibility, because you are fighting for them.

We clean the city all day. Our duty is from 6 am to 12 noon. We do clean the whole city by 9:30, 10:00. After that it is impossible, to clean the roads because of vehicular traffic, people and all. But you go and see. You go and see the Park Street condition now, you go and see in front of Grand Hotel, situation is the worst. Anybody can say there is no waste collection system in Kolkata. But we do remove daily average 3500 to 4500 metric tons of solid waste everyday. You see how much we have cleaned yesterday? 4136 metric tons of waste by 351 vehicles. But after seeing the city, can you say that there is a department of waste management that cleans the city? You will say, no there is no such department. This is also frustrating for me. I am not against hawker, but what they are doing is not good. They should control themselves. They should do their business but they should not throw their waste on the streets.

The citizens buy from the hawker because they sit there. But if you ask the citizens: do you want these hawkers? They will say: No. The shop owners, those who pay tax everyday, they don't want them.

The population increase in India is very high, that is the problem. And that leads to economic problems and so on. Unless you control this, we will have all other problems the next thousand years.

In the city now there is a tendency to have only one or two children. But in villages you will find no restrictions, four, five, six children. Even we have some employees in our corporation that have many children. I know a person who has 20 children, and three wives. This is the main issue. The issue is not the hawker. It is true, who wants to be a hawker? It is not a good, a prestigious job.

I am not against the poor people. They are Indian we live in the same country. But some discipline should be there. The HSC is not really getting the regulation through. But if we as KMC and the police take action against them they say, we are inhuman and so on. But the city is for everybody, not only the hawker. I think our corporation has done a very good job. We are allowing them to do their thing, but maintaining the policy.

The city situation has gotten better. Roads have improved, waste management has improved, shopping malls are coming up, flyovers and everything. The infrastructural side is improving very fast. The IT sector is slowly becoming number one in the country. So the city is doing well. Businessmen want to come, even the foreign investors.

Only one thing we have not done, that is family planning. Since Independence nobody tried to control the population otherwise we have everything. Whatever you do now it is difficult to control. Because if you construct now say 100 new industries in India, you still cannot tackle this.

Typology: Hairdressers

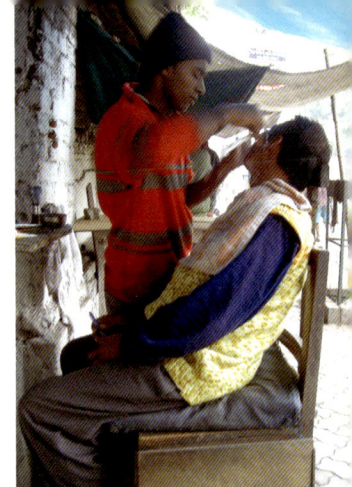

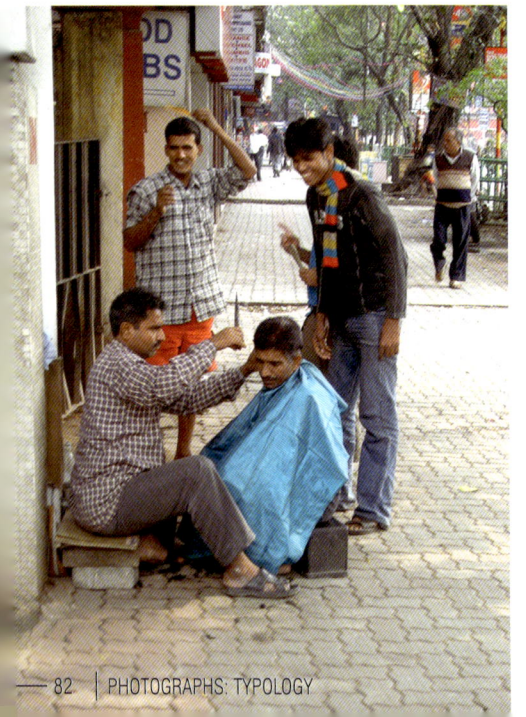

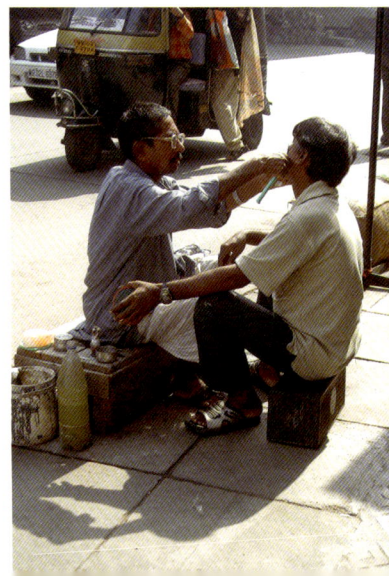

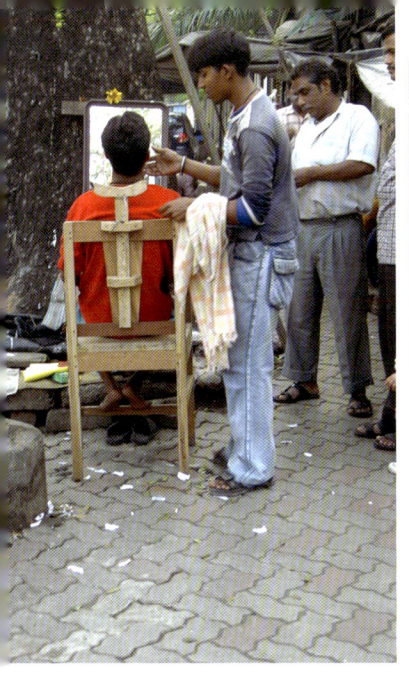

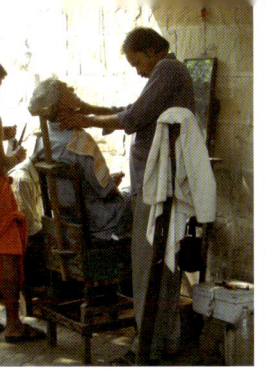

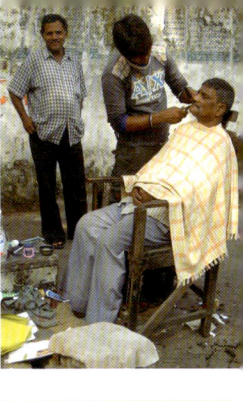

Interview Transcripts

10 Manish Chakrabarti, Architect

Calcutta is quite a big city; about forty million people divided among various sections and communities: Bengalis, non-Bengalis including people from different parts of India. And divided into two major religions, Hindu and Muslim, and there is kind of a community which grew in different locations. The Muslims more or less stay in a certain area, the Chinese stay in another area, as do the Bengalis. Of course there's been a mixture of these communities over a long period of time. What is interesting is that Kolkata is essentially a trading post. It flourished as a trading city. The huge amount of jobs and opportunities that opened up with the arrival of the English 300 years ago, and with the emergence of the present Kolkata, people got attracted to it. It became a primary city with respect to other neighbouring states. People from Orissa, Bihar come here in search of jobs and opportunities. What is interesting about a trading city is that it is a tertiary city. It remains as a tertiary city for a long time now... where it is very difficult to understand the economics of the tertiary sector. How much the city earns itself per day is very difficult to grasp. And this earning happens at almost every corner. Whether in a private space, in an office, over fax and telephones or emails, or whether actually physically trading with some material against cash. And that happens at every corner, on the road, the footpaths, on the streets. It is kind of an aspiring city for the many people. It gives space to many people to earn their own living and that is fascinating, because city is all about that, city is all about creating chances and opportunities.

In that way, many cities in the developing world, in India and elsewhere, more or less share the same phenomena. It is about the tertiary sector, about the informal sector which keeps the city going. That is very important to understand and realize because the

economic base of a city is proportionate too: the primary sector, the secondary sector, and it is a function of the tertiary sector itself.

So the informal sector is very important. It is very abundantly available and unfortunately there are not many efforts in understanding, organising, grouping this sector. It is very difficult and understood even less. How can you track down who has a relationship with whom? And who has sold what to whom?

Kolkata was mentioned as a dying city by the then Prime Minister Rajiv Gandhi, about 15 years ago. It did not die. Rajiv Gandhi did not understand the role of the tertiary sector, the informal sector. A city can die if it doesn't have a tertiary - an informal sector. I look at this as an opportunity, as an asset rather than a liability. It only needs to be understood and organised as much as possible. Not to play the role of a planner or an urban strategist and solving it, rather to enable them to perform the important role of this economic base. Enabling them to flourish more and to find their own ways of graduating from an informal sector to a more permanent sector.

It is not a paradox that the municipal agencies or the town planners do not realize this problem. It happens almost everywhere. It is very dificult to realize that you have a gem in your family. Often you don't tend to recognize the gem that sits by your side. So I think the municipality doesn't realize the huge potential that this particular unorganized sector holds for the city.

But at large I think that the concept of plannning is changing. There has been a big drive to remove hawkers from their places and so forth. But I think hawkers are going to stay, are going to live. So it is important to plan for them rather than evicting them. As I said not a master planning but a strategic planning. Rather than freezing hawkers into a certain location. Enabling them to move places and hawk from one place to the other and only concentrating myself on people who trade on the streets. There are a lot of people who don't trade on the street but just lurk around.

I exist in both these realms of private buildings and public clients.

I have realized one thing, that if you try to do things on your own, it does influence at some point of time the quarters who need to understand these matters. It happened in a few of my projects, which is unlike a very client-architect relationship. Where the client is a community, the client is a city. One can look into that but it becomes a bit out of hand and out of proportion. So such efforts which I have undertaken earlier tend to inform a larger audience with various degrees of understanding and misunderstanding. But it does inform. Perhaps we are a little changed in the city of today, in the city of Kolkata, in the city of the world, I think this has happened because of various engagements, where various people in this larger context, such as professionals like me, have informed the government, the decisionmakers, who have taken a note of it or they have not taken a note of it. Of the things they have taken a note of, they try to translate to policy, or make it a paradigm of politics and so on. But what is interesting, is that today a client is a much more educated client than earlier. I say educated because information is much easier to gain than it used to be earlier. Even for a person who is not in the upper brackets of society it is possible to access information. And therefore it is a much more enlightened underprivileged class which can become the client of a professional.

If we think of the city as a collection of many small communities, many small jurisdictions or constituencies, I think that each of them can articulate what they want for themselves. And that can be a brief for a client. It is a way of an utopian but also not very utopian thinking. Some things are already happening on the ground on these manners but it can be extended. Architecture, urban planning, a conservation practice can be thought of as increasingly towards that direction. You no longer get projects falling onto your drawing board, you try to create projects. When you talk about an urban level scale of a project like recently I was called by the

Municipal Corporation to look into one of the burning ghat areas. And there are two: one in the south and one in the north. And at the one in the north they used the traditional Hindu method to burn bodies with wood. And depending on how rich you are, you would have actually used sandalwood, so it brings some fragrance. They are essentially conducted by a community called '*doms*'. They do that particular function. And they are hired by the local municipal corporation, they are paid on a monthly basis and they have an accommodation which is under a little bit of a danger. That was the point of interest of the municipality, this is where politics comes in, the sense of insecurity comes in, worried about people saying bad things about the municipality. That is the point when they intervene. And they wanted to intervene so they brought me there. They wanted to see how this could be repaired or renewed or revived etcetera,. as well as a kind of a general aggregation of the location, of the shops that are on the other side of the footpath, how do you reorganise the shop, how do you communicate with them, how do you conduct the uses, how do you bring them into a kind of a participatory situation? Participation is very difficult. People never participate. People have to be made to participate. How do you do that? How honestly do you do that? That is more important.

I think it is more difficult but it is an increasingly happening thing not only in a city like Kolkata which is a developing city, but in many developing cities across the world.

Typology: Street Architecture

Typology: Street Situations

Interview Transcripts

11 Bonani Kakkar, People United for Better Living In Calcutta

 There is a funny story to tell. The KMC commissioner was supposed to go to a conference from Eisenhower fellowship. On his name board it said Alapan Bandyopadhay and then they listed him as the president of the hawkers association. Because that man too was invited to the same conference. So they put him as the municipal commissioner and switched it around. That was quite amusing.

We, meaning just a small group of concerned people, started a couple of years ago. In Kolkata there are many concerned people but we do a lot of complaining but we don't act. So our group decided to keep it small as we don't have to get things passed by large meetings or a committee. If we decide to act on something, we sometimes just have a round of phone calls and we move. So we had to be cohesive. We believe that things can be changed.

The core value we have is: things have to be addressed, the government has to listen to stakeholders. We can't say we represent all of Kolkata but we represent a viewpoint. Some NGOs say we are not reaching ground level, we are not reaching the poor. But we just bring our views to the table, that is what we decided on.

The CPM branded us as people living in high-rise buildings and AC comfort talking about environment. But today I must say that after all these years we are at the table deciding on some very important issues for the city. If there is a public hearing, the announcement is just put in the newspaper. But to make sure they have participation, they will invite us to be at the meeting.

We are mostly concerned about the environment of Kolkata. There is a whole range of problems in the city. We were experiencing power-cuts, telephones weren't working. That's when we decided that we wanted to provide a platform, harness all the anger of people who feel things should improve.

It was maybe six or seven years ago that the KMC and the police jointly started an operation called Operation Sunshine. And the hawkers were removed from 22 major streets. On that issue we were supportive of that move to limit the access of the hawkers to those streets. Because there was very heavy traffic, like Rash Behari Avenue, and the entire place was taken up by hawkers and wasn't as you see now, that they were just vending. They had actually constructed stalls and some of them were living on top. And also the shop owners on that street had problems, people couldn't even see the shops anymore, didn't have access. Also the sewage lines were under those pavements. And because it was occupied they could not clean that.

The municipal commissioner wanted our views. So we said they should be allowed to sell their things but hawking doesn't mean a permanent place. That place has been designated as a sidewalk, for people to walk. If they spill over to the carriage way it's very dangerous. Especially I am talking about Gariahat corner, because there is a lot of traffic. There were quite a few accidents. But when the hawkers were removed from there and they were given space, a lot of them didn't want to. But for at least a year, or a year and a half those roads, the pavements were really clear. But then they got political backing from Mamata Banerjee of Trinamul Congress and they came right back. So as it stands now, we have some pavements that are again completely blocked. And we have used a calendar as a giveaway for the government people. The calendar would be on the issues that we feel are worth thinking about. If the government had solved the problem we put a button on the back and write about it. And if they failed in doing anything that issue was also taken up. So when we actually went to take photographs, they actually chased our photographer and said it is because of people like you that the police comes after us.

We think the issue has to be regulated: enough space for pedestrians and no allowance for constructing stalls. A lot of our municipal commissioners visit our neighbouring countries. There is the same thing in Thailand or in other countries. But it is controlled. But here it became a right. So as soon as they got a space they felt as if it didn't matter whether for the pedestrians, the city service, whether it is a water drain that had to be cleaned, they wouldn't give up that space. We saw it as a very militant attitude among the hawkers. We didn't deal with the hawkers union, only with the government. But we feel that they have to give in a little and move back.

But the present mayor, when he came into office, all the hawkers came back. Because the elections came and they control a lot of votes with the association, the hawkers were not removed. The mayor just drew a yellow line for how far the hawkers could occupy the pavement. But if you go to Dalhousie Square, where there is a designated heritage site, it is full of hawkers. So some regulation has to come: to occupy just a part of the pavement and only stay there for a certain time.

But we know that the hawkers do have problems. When they widen the street for example as in Park Street, There were very old beautiful trees. And we were trying very hard to save at least one side of the streets from the trees being cut. We almost succeeded but later in the night the KMC came and cut it off. Students who worked with us went to interview the people that were working under those trees: a barber, and a man with his ironing table called a "dhopa', also sitting there. "Other people have air-conditioned offices. This tree was giving me all the shelter and this is the place for the waking hours of the day, this is my place of work. So with the tree gone I don't know where to go and I don't know how to carry on my business. Everybody has a space. And this was my space".

We are not pro-hakwers. But we believe there is space for everyone if you use the pavements you have to do it in such a manner that you don't restrict pedestrians. And there has to be some regard on safety regulations. But this is also a political problem. In some places they take water to prepare the food, which may not be very pure. So we were talking to the KMC since you know there are these food stalls, why don't you put a clean source of piped water there? They say: that's encouraging the food hawkers. If you do that then we are giving our stamp of approval.

Sometimes it is the failing of large companies not to provide a cafeteria for their workers. For the very high ranking people, like in Tata Centre, the bearers wear white gloves and come and serve the food. But for the lower ranks at Tata Centre, these people have nothing else to do but go around the corner and eat on the streets. So it is the collective responsibility of the corporate sector as well.

So something has to be done. Kolkata has only 4% open space. We don't want more areas given to the hawkers. There is an office at the corner of Park Street and there is a gentleman who is a very important person in the Chamber of Commerce. But he says, I am not interested in doing anything for the city anymore, I don't want my children to be in this city. Because I can't get off my car and approach my office as that entire space is occupied by hawkers. So it has got to do with the image of the city as well. A lot of large companies feel that this city is no longer a city where you can conduct business, it has become a place for an influx of people from Bihar. In the area near Brabourne Road, there is not a single person who is from Bengal. They are coming in because we have a good railway system. Kolkata has been proud in taking in everybody, we don't want to be like the Shiv Sena. But it is coming, we think, to a breaking point.

Here, there is the willingness to do something, take initiative. The poor don't depend on government and handouts. But yet some policy has to come into place that they don't blunt civic services, the pavements. In Kolkata the pavements are shrinking. In a city in which just by walking a short distance you could do a lot of things, it is now changing. Car factories being set up in India, new flyovers are being built, the middle class moving up, so for the new lot of personal cars they are widening the roads. There is a municipal law which says how wide a pavement is, and in some areas like after the new Park Street area the flyover comes down going to a bridge. That used to be a wide pavement. The people usually walk there, when they get off the train. But when the pavement disappears, what will they do? But they had to make the street wider because the Japanese government gave the funds. But they only give money to build flyovers and superhighways as they have done elsewhere in the world, because they want their cars to be imported, or they set up a factory. So we need better public transport instead of more cars, whether it be a Japanese or a Tata car.

Typology: Standby

Typology: Repair & Production

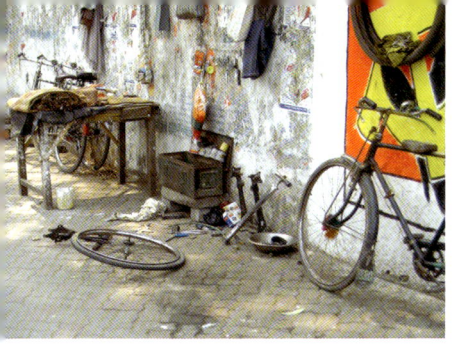

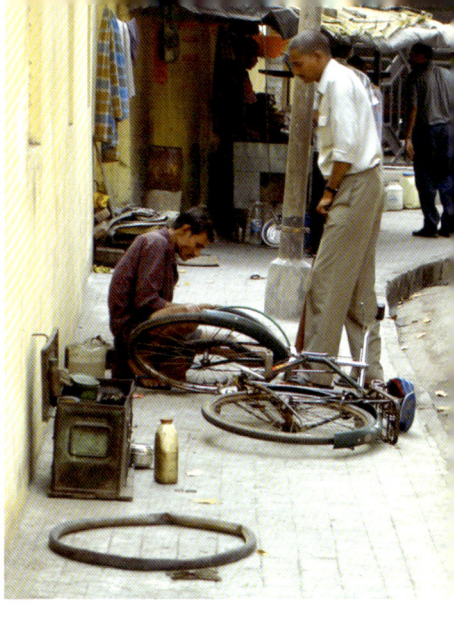

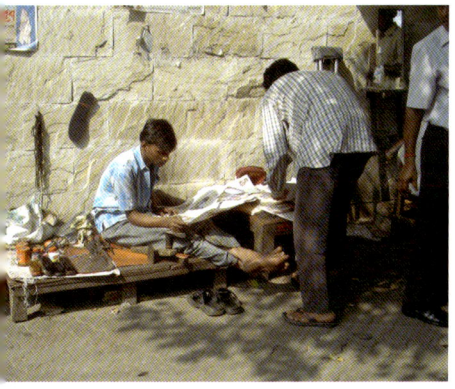

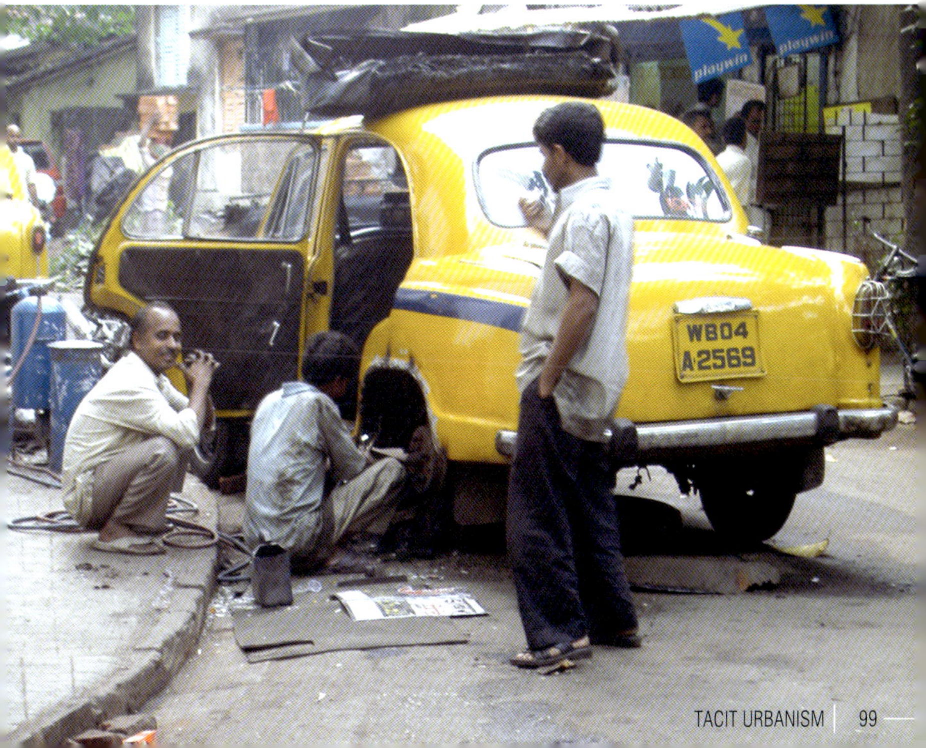
playwin
playwin
WB04
A·2569

Typology: Newspapers

Typology: Writing

Typology: Transport

Typology: Transport

Typology: Selling

Typology: Mixed Use

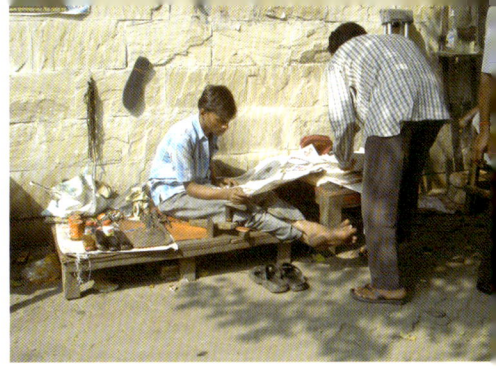

Typology: Mixed Use

Kolkata Monodosis: Project documentation

Inspired by the diverse and exciting social life on Kolkata's pavements (owing much to the cultural practice of the hawkers who occupy it), I decided to do a project in the streets. I picked up my concept of Monodosis, which is a research on musical form and converted it into an urban space intervention.

My intention was to use Monodosis as a kind of performative plug-in to the city, which reacts to the specific situation and at the same time, provokes interaction with the everyday pedestrians and hawkers.

How is that done? Very simple: a solo improvising vibraphone meets urban space production. From that point on, cultural practice starts to work in various dimensions. A performative research on form, material, energy and transformation emerges.

Since we chose ten locations, scouted by Patrick Ghose, the project could also be interpreted as a portrait of Kolkata: it works in different spaces, different levels of society, different economic layers. Even the instrument I use is Kolkata-specific: it is the only vibraphone in the city. In the 50s it was brought in by Victor Feldman (who later became pianist with Miles Davis), and given to Antonio Menezes, a protagonist of the then thriving Calcutta jazz scene of the 50s, 60s and early 70s. He later constructed a frame for the instrument, enabling him to carry it around more easily. In fact, this effect came in very handy for our endeavor, .

While making the project, we realized that it works on many different levels. Since my way of playing is very different to the culture of Kolkata, we observed an alienation effect, which opened up experience. People could react directly to the musical performance without having to label it. The reactions could vary from nodding the head to the rhythm of the music, to video capturing the performance with a mobile phone, to asking questions on the performance, to telling friends what is happing or just passing by, ignoring what is happening.

After each performance a dialogue with the audience unfolded. The question that came up the most was: Why do you do this? What is your aim? And while this question is asked, the answer is already given. The intention of Kolkata Monodosis is to raise questions on today's practice, on the use of urban space. To ask what is formal and what is informal, what is use or misuse, what is public and non-public and so on. So with this project I want to expand creativity, allowing space for alternate perspectives on, and readings of the urban. Perspectives that drive beyond the mere application of forms but intends to encourage the reflection on how and why forms are created.

In that way Monodosis becomes a kind of performative meta-practice which puts improvisation into the focus. Improvisation as interaction in real-time, as constructive use of disorder in a transforming community. As Joseph Beuys expanded the notion of fine arts to arrive at the "soziale Plastik", the Kolkata Monodosis project could stand for an 'expanded' way to interpret musical practice. By widening the aspects of music in this project, we arrive at a social technology that I would like to call improvisation technology.

Improvisation technology is about organisation of space in time, it is about using economy not as a given but as an asset. It strives to enable to perform, to inform and to provoke reflection on form. I hope that Improvisation Technology can open up new ways of reading and appropriating urban space in the future.

Once we started the project, everybody got deeply involved in the making process.

Producing the film with Ranu Ghosh, Patrick Ghose and Abdul Rajjak. is thus not merely to be seen as a one-to-one capturing of the street interventions.

The cooperation of the film team is a creative interdisciplinary process in itself, which on a meta-production level, stands for an artistic endeavor of finding an experimental form of, and for its own. In this way it is opening yet another level, another dimension of possibilities for interpretations, for readings of the totality of the project.

Christopher Dell

Kolkata

13/02/08

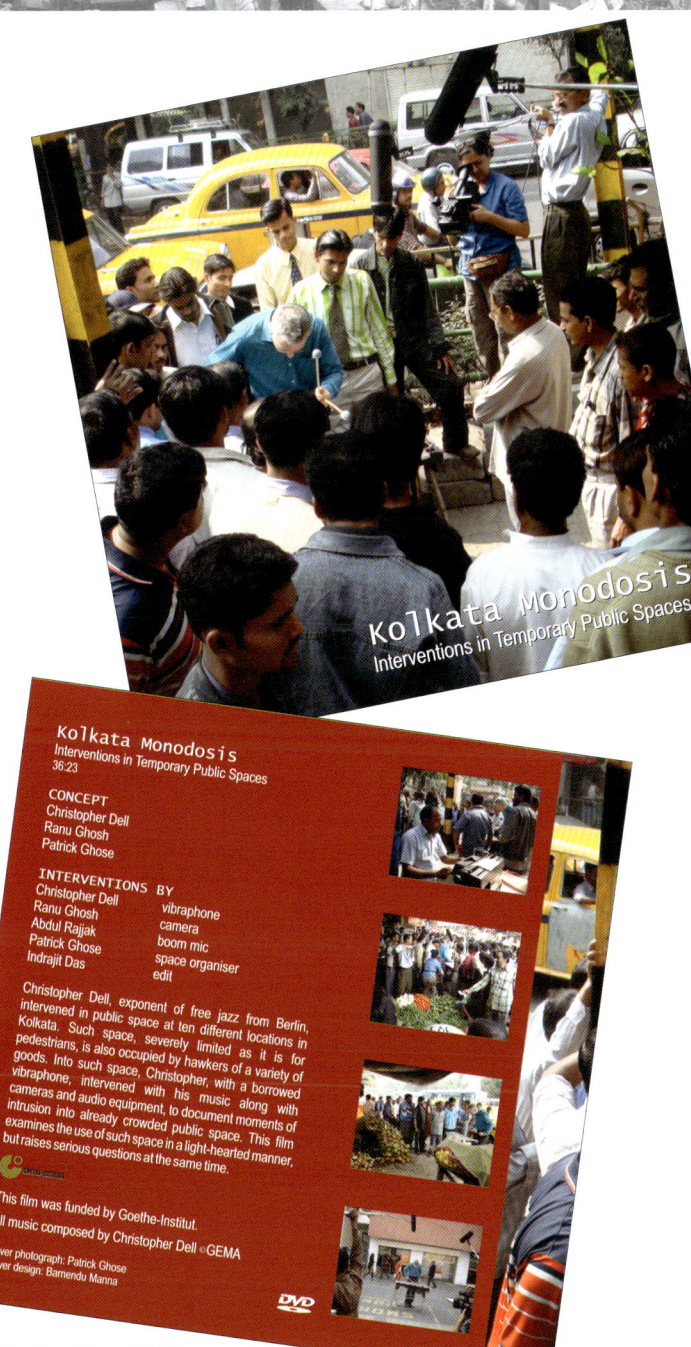

Kolkata Monodosis
Interventions in Temporary Public Spaces

Kolkata Monodosis
Interventions in Temporary Public Spaces
36:23

CONCEPT
Christopher Dell
Ranu Ghosh
Patrick Ghose

INTERVENTIONS BY
Christopher Dell
Ranu Ghosh   vibraphone
Abdul Rajjak   camera
Patrick Ghose   boom mic
Indrajit Das   space organiser
                      edit

Christopher Dell, exponent of free jazz from Berlin, intervened in public space at ten different locations in Kolkata. Such space, severely limited as it is for pedestrians, is also occupied by hawkers of a variety of goods. Into such space, Christopher, with a borrowed vibraphone, intervened with his music along with cameras and audio equipment, to document moments of intrusion into already crowded public space. This film examines the use of such space in a light-hearted manner, but raises serious questions at the same time.

This film was funded by Goethe-Institut.
All music composed by Christopher Dell ©GEMA

Cover photograph: Patrick Ghose
Cover design: Barnendu Manna

DVD

Facsimile of the DVD cover

Kolkata Monodosis: Project documentation

Patrick S L Ghose: *Text and Photographs*

None of the locations are completely representative of the city, nor were they intended to be, but then again, as a senior police officer told us in a different context, "the sum of the parts is greater than the whole".

Christopher and Ranu Ghosh, the cinematographer, viewed my suggested options over a couple of days and we were agreed. Sealdah came out of a suggestion from the Hawker Sangram Committee, and Christopher had already been inspired by Park Street and Gariahat on an earlier visit. These were places I would have suggested anyway. The choices were clear; and we felt this even during our scouting expeditions, quite ideal.

We thought of the first, or opening scene, to be quite literally that. The opening up, an awakening. The Oberoi Grand Hotel arcade on Chowringhee Road is a long, covered public space dotted with the flimsy architecture of street-side stalls draped in plastic held fast by jute and nylon twine, waiting to display their wares. This particular pathway, otherwise most busy, is a sort of no-man's land at nine in the morning. The office-rushing crowds tend to bypass it, the big shops are yet to open, and the street vendors are still having a tea and a peaceful smoke before they get down to unpacking their goods for the steady stream of itinerant shoppers who will soon fill that space to overflowing in a couple of hours.

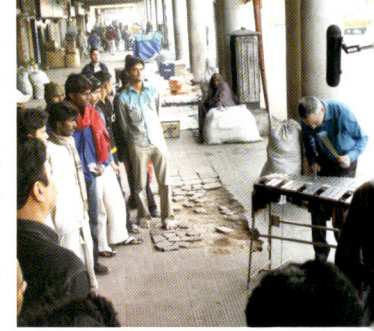

The street in front of the Park Street Post Office is milling with pedestrians, mostly office goers. The street stationers and typist provide convenient services for the the thousands who throng the postal department as well as for nearby offices urgently out-of-stock with envelopes or sticky tape.

At 10 am Dalhousie Square, BBD Bagh, is just gearing up for another day at the office. Netaji Subhas Road at the Duncan House corner bifurcates with one road going straight down to the Brabourne Road flyover and the other

taking a sharp turn towards Strand Road. Christopher's performance at this V-junction attracted a crowd of enthusiastic listeners who were reluctant to let him go.

The Shyambazar 5-point crossing is the main junction of north Kolkata. Five major roads leading in almost all directions of the compass converge at the ugly gilded statue of Netaji Subhas Chandra Bose astride a horse, which for reasons known only to the sculptor, has its tail sticking straight out and horizontal. At 11 in the morning it is a scene of organised chaos, and the noise levels have gone beyond pain to a dull awareness which is almost organic. People still have time to stop and stare no matter where they are rushing to or from. A recurrent element at nearly every location. The policeman on duty

at this crossing came over after 15 minutes and very politely requested us to wrap it up and move on before we caused more havoc to traffic than he wanted to cope with. We readily agreed.

Babughat is a major ferry jetty on the central Kolkata side for those crossing the river. Under a young banyan tree, the coconut vendor

placidly regards Christopher with no surprise. But this is a buzzing transit station, and not many have the time or inclination to listen to music before they go on to wherever it is they need to go.

Kumartuli in the north is as much a cliché of Kolkata as it is an endearing aspect of this city's cultural ethos. In this small colony of clay idol makers, images of the goddess Saraswati, (she the muse of learning and music, so significant to a citizenry who pride themselves as constituents of a "knowledge society"),

and whose celebrations are only days away, line the alleys in various stages of finish. Almost all the establishments here are semi-permanent structures which could easily be street stalls on a pavement somewhere else.

Christopher performs in a yellow outlined box decorated with a trash bin in a corner, designated "Smoking Zone" on the pavement

outside the City Centre shopping mall in Salt Lake. The pavement borders an even wider carriageway, on the other side of which are hawker stalls selling only things to eat, drink, smoke or chew. A sign advertising underwear atop the police assistance booth across the street urges one to "Live like a Macro Man".

If you aren't expecting it, the hustle and bustle of frenetic commerce under the flyover that spans past the Sealdah station complex can come as a cultural shock. There's a section here where commuter village women sell amazingly fresh vegetables and fruit. The density of pedestrian traffic here laughs mockingly at any rule about personal space. Intersperse this with hand-pulled rickshaws and cycle vans and you may well wonder if our sanity should come under scrutiny to film Christopher's performance right there.

Sunset by the river is one of the best times in a Kolkata day. The walkway, commonly called the Strand, between the waters of the Hooghly and the railway lines that separate it from the road, also spoils you with a choice of delicious street food to feed the hunger that comes as you watch the evening sun go down behind the Second Hooghly Bridge.

Gariahat is south Calcutta's prime junction. Wider pavements than Shyambazar give space to an abundance of street stalls. Bag and garment sellers, crockery and glassware vie for the attention of office workers

returning home past established shops selling expensive sarees. Brightly lit by advertising signs and street lights, this was Christopher's only after-dark performance and intervention. It was also the last shoot. A distinct sense of closure.

For more photos of the making of Kolkata Monodosis,
visit: http://picasaweb.com/pslghose/kolkatamonodosis

Synthesis

Urban Governance

Urban governance in the last fifteen years has been concentrating on economic liberalisation. Linking India with the global economy led to a massive inflow of capital from outside the country and also to a rise in indigenous investment. It was the aim to increase employment within or around urban centres. Although many jobs were created, to a much larger extent jobs have been cut off in the formal sector, leading to an extreme increase in the informal sector over the past years. The strategy of keeping budgetary deficits low also led to a low rate of infrastructural investment. As an effect of this, we observe a destabilisation of the agrarian economy, causing high unemployment in rural areas which then again leads to rapid urban growth.

At the present time it is obvious, that an urban strategy based solely on the organized sector is not viable on account of its limited capacity to create employment and income for the lower classes. It has been stated by the local municipality, that as soon as they change the strategy towards the hawkers as a development that emphasises the informal organisation, this may lead to encouraging even more of them to crowd the pavements. But the truth is, that is happening anyway.

The HSC estimates that about 75% of the local workforce are working in the informal sector, many of them migrants from rural areas, who come into the city for the day and go back in the evening. Some stay in the city over the week and go home to the village for a day. As we learned, hawking is not isolated in the urban center. There is a high proportion of women home workers, who, in small production units, produce goods which are then sold in the city. Usually these goods are cheaper than the goods that come through retail markets like Burrabazar. Here goods from Mumbai, Delhi and other cities are sold. Because many middlemen are involved, these goods are costlier. In this way, hawking functions as an outlet for the region's local, small scale productivity.

The eastern periphery of Kolkata has been witnessing significant transformations giving way to intensive housing investments for the upper and middle classes. New projects continue to develop along the bypass including five-star hotels, elite residential complexes, private hospitals and sites for leisure activities. These units are isolated and their connection with the city is causing huge traffic problems. At the same time, we see the widening of streets, the reduction of public space, the construction of barricaded parks by private agencies, the increase in personalised motor transport infrastructure which is accompanied by a decline in public transport. This can be interpereted as a manifestation of a dualistic concept of urban planning instead of a strategy for heterogenous cross-society development.

Low-income housing, as well as organisation issues of the city center itself such as traffic, waste managment, etc. have been neglected. The exclusionist agenda of urban growth without resettlement or rehabilitation urges the oustees to migrate to the center and work there on the pavement.

Rajiv Gandhi once stated, that Kolkata is a dying city. One of the reasons why it is not dying lies in the thriving informal sector and its continuing interaction with the rural hinterland. Circular migration remains a strong aspect, providing a low-capital production network in periods of decline in formal employment.

At the same time it has to be stated, that hostile policy environment is also due to the fact, that hawking causes traffic congestion, accidents, health hazards and problems for shop owners, who depend on pedestrian traffic.

Taking these factors into account, it seems obvious that there is a need to explicitly recognise the role of the informal sector in development plans. This holds especially true for the hawkers, since they work in the open public spaces. This implies a political economy of change in the planning and management of the city.

Policy shift

In Kolkata the liberalisation policy, together with the decline of the industrial sector, saw a massive growth in hawking over the last 30 years. Nonetheless, it was only with the National Policy that hawking came into the ambit of local policy. Right now, with the foundation of the Apex Committee, we can observe a policy shift from eviction and/or relocation of hawkers towards regulation of hawking. That leads to a more systematic, integrated approach that takes into account the various interests in the city. Three major players are involved: the Kolkata Municipal Corporation, the Police and the hawker umbrella organisation, Hawker Sangram Committee.

The role of the architect in this scope, as Manish Chakraborty states, is the enabler, the one who in small scale projects contributes to both formal and informal measures that can moderate the urban process. Thus the central task of city management is to provide a framework for a dynamic trasformation not only for global financial or IT businesses but also for the local low-capital, informal economies. This is not only tied to physical measures but also to a change of legal structures and politics.

The impact that globalisation had on urban governance is mostly seen as a liberation for cities, as a lifting of tight national control that made them dependent on national policy. But as we see, in the case of Kolkata's hawkers it worked in just the opposite way. It was the National Policy which made local change possible.

Henri Lefebvre rightly asserts, that "physical land is not just a means of production but a part of the forces of production".[1] Physical space in Kolkata is under pressure: increase of prices for residential

---

[1] Lefebvre, Henri, *The Production of Space*, Oxford 1991

as well as business space, and with only 4% of public space and 6% of road space.

In the hawker issue and the negotiation on open public space that goes along with it, we can observe how governmental techniques of controlling society become highly physical. It also shows the critical importance of everyday fighting that one finds connected to the making and unmaking of the urban. The conflict of urban space shows that neither does the secret of politics lie solely in certain political configurations of the everyday, nor is politics led solely by laws, commands and institutions. The materiality of the process shows, that politics is conducted by the combination of these two, by a dialectical movement.

Working on the urban is essentially a matter of understanding form. Not as reduction of built form but as expansion to the form of politics, problematizing the notion of form in the context of politics, because forms are the concrete problems politics engages with. In the case of the hawker it is clear that a small formal change in the National Policy can have a big impact. The example also shows how a group that formerly had no voice, tries to make itself heard in the political arena, in entering form, in trying to bridge the gap between the informal and the formal.

Hannah Arendt once said, "in order to enjoy rights, we require the right to have rights". This is a highly formal question. In the case of the hawkers, the fight for acknowlegdement, for being legalised means the yearning to converse anew, beyond pre-established procedure of form. When the German social scientist Jürgen Habermas says, that there is nothing to invent, that we can only conserve the gains, he certainly is concerned about already achieved normative benefits such as social security etc. But when this is only true for a certain group of the society, how do you go about that? And how do you anticipate structural changes, for example in the economic sector?

What we conclude is that the complex interplay of political, social and cultural factors cannot be reduced to a single narrative of city-planning. As the hawkers are still in the state of 'permanent exception'. But they, together with the Apex Committee, are working on a way to find a form for the informal, to strip off uncertainty to a certain extent and become legally definable in terms of licence, retirement plans, spacing.

The complex economic and social movement of the city, the territoral expansion of hawkers on one side, the widening of streets, and implementation of flyovers on the other side obliges the public officials to consider "right-sizing", if only tacitly. Governing a city is the task of governing population, governing resources and so forth. They become interlinked tasks of governing a territory. A space that has so many other forms: ethnic, cultural, economic, geographical etc., aquires a territorial form. As a process of politics nothing can be more material than this. And the Hawker Policy of Kolkata shows it very clearly.

The power to effect the spatial reorganization is invoked in the name of a National Policy, and as yet there is little alternative to policymaking as a form of regulation, though regulation requires both self-regulation and a legal form. The need for the inclusion of form for the hawkers, grows out of their quest for legitimacy, the desire to invoke public authority. In this context, they have to connect to a familiar order, which is provided by the government and the police, and transform it to a new policy. Although this tactic may prove costly to the hawker unions by denying them the strategic thrust or 'war of movement', it at the same time takes nothing away from their agency. The regular meetings of the Apex Committee, educational moves by the union as well as awareness-drives by the KMC point out that a new specific governance-pattern seems to be evolving.

Manuel Castels and others have indicated, that the urban is becoming a free-floating network. While this notion holds true to a large extent, it is also important to acknowledge that the urban is regulated by normative settings. The hawker debate in Kolkata shows how these normative settings cannot be taken for granted, but are a matter of permanent negotiation. This is essentially a matter of form and the criticising of form.

One of the problems lies in the fact that over time, forms tend to be applied rather than be reflected upon. This then becomes a hegemonial practice: established forms, orders, are naturalized and legitimised through their existence without reflecting upon the conflict that went along with the form's constitution. One of the implications of this is that the truth of form lies in its liminal nature. That is why criticising form is no empty formalism; it is a way to understand how politics work s and how it creates order.

Cultural studies have exhaustingly studied modes of representation, now this has to be combined with studying action. Cultural explanation of politics provides only a partial understanding of the politics of the city, while liberal theories professing good governance are at the same time too synthetic to be acceptable and too closed up in interpreting the global market as a natural law. In such a context, there arises the need for a dialectical approach to emphasise the physicality of politics and the political dimension of physicality. Built environment and everyday interaction are then seen as an active production of the urban in which we participate, whether we want to or not. In this way, studying the tacit urbanism, and making explicit the tacit political and cultural levels of the urban becomes an important part of not only understanding the urban as a totality, but also of how we act as citizens and how we participate in the constitution of urban structure.

There is no such thing as neutral space.

Appendix

Scans of interesting and relevant documents

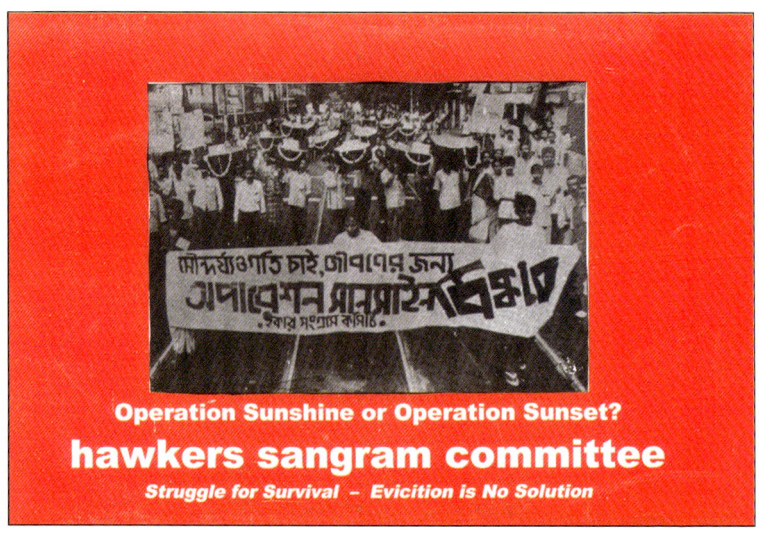

SEEKING SUSTAINABLE SUPPORT

- Considering the fact that all the costs of such a long movement has been raised by the limited contribution of the direct members
- It is imperative that we raise resources from all concerned persons
- Contributions in Indian Currency may be made in favour 'Calcutta Hawker Sangram Samity' payable at Kolkata
- Foreign Contributions may be made by demand draft or cheques drawn in favour of "BADE KHANTURA BAHUMUKHI SEVA KENDRA" FCRA No. 147110407 drawn on Bank of India, Khantura Branch SB/CA Account No. 7645

HAWKERS SANGRAM COMMITTEE
Struggle for Survival

Hawkers Sangram Committee (A Struggle for Street Vendors), (HSC) - is a totally spontaneous struggle that has sustained for about a decade on support generated by self motivated activists for the cause.

With its beginning in Kolkata, West Bengal, India HSC has now had a snowball efect where larger human rights issues have become a part of its existence.

While Liberalisation, Privaisation & Globalisation (LPG) is considered the most progressive need for the Urban Poor we in practice feel that it is as lethal as the otherwise commonly known LPG (Liquid Petroleum Gas).

In the experience of HSC - now in its 7th year of struggle have closely worked with the vast majority has faced a severe struggles that has changed the way of life for the common person.

On that fateful night HSC has faced - fighting shoulder to shoulder with the poor is the midnight 24th November 1996 in the Northern part of the city of Kolkata - when in the name of **'development ...... disaster were justified......** by demolishing and physically beating.... up several slum dwellers amongst whom street vendors were vast majority.

The effect of single night was such that its effect were seen well till the beginning of the next year..... none of us have been able to forget and still relive the loot, arson, and fire that was done with all possible physical force with Para military forces..water jets, tear gas and baton beating.

HSC since its incpetion has been contnuing its fight for human rights of persons who form the 'pavement economy' - who constantly face the threat of eviction by the law enforcing bodies and arms of the State.

The entire operation for the state machinery was known as "operation Sunshine" while for us in our demonstrations it was known as 'Operation Sunset"

Needless to say, as in most third world economies - the informal sector is the only manner where the vast majority finds its survival.

Vision

To turn our dream of a just society where the actual implementation of human development is directed care and concern for the Pavement Economy Population for whom eviction and insecurity is the order of the day.

Mission

To continue to struggle till such time that all persons compelled to a Pavement Existence are assured of a life of safety. security and dignity.

Objectives

* To organise the informal sector trade
* To campaign and lobby towards permanent status with due licensing
* To eradicate unscrupulous indebtedness
* To ensure education, shelter and housing rights
* To ensure justice an 1 given informed choices regarding any large urban developmental plans.
* To create lobbying. campaigns, and act as a pressure groups nationally and internationally.
* To create a Resource Centre for Research, Law and create a complete understanding that **Eviction is No Solution**

FUTURE PLANS

- International Resource Mobilization on the sharing of best practises with regard to informal sector
- Networking with other International Movements
- To create a collective Watch Dog on Evictions without acceptable alternatives
- Consider Gender Issues in Vending & Resettlement
- Seeking solutions for alternative national economies threatened by Globalisation

HAWKERS SANGRAM COMMITTEE

16/17, College Street, Kolkata - 700 012
Phone : (O) 91-33-2196688, Fax : 91-33-5316484
Email - shaktimanghosh@hotmail.com/shaktiman2001@pioneerbizz.com
This Publicaiton is courtesy SPAN - Society for Peoples Awareness, 66/2 Sarat Chandra Dhar Road, P.O. Noapara, Kolkata - 700 090
and Bade Khantura, Bahumukhi Seva Kendra, Vill : Bade Khantura, Dist : 24 Pgs. (North), Pin - 743273, West Bengal

NATIONAL POLICY
ON
URBAN STREET VENDORS

Department of Urban Employment & Poverty Alleviation
Ministry of Urban Development & Poverty Alleviation
Government of India

2004

Personal Assistant
to the Mayor

THE KOLKATA MUNICIPAL CORPORATION
5, S. N. Banerjee Road, Kolkata - 700 013
Off. Ph : 2286 1211, 2286 1000 Ext : 2155
Fax : 2291 11, 2286 1211

No.   07 - 06 - 2006.

Secretary,
Hawkers Sangram Committee,
16/17, College Street,
<u>Kolkata - 700 012.</u>

S i r,

    As directed, Minutes of the meeting held in the Chamber
of Hon'ble Mayor on 22nd February, 2006 with different Hawkers
Unions in connection with Hawker's issue is enclosed herewith
for your ready reference please.

                                  Yours faithfully,

                                 08/6/06
Enclo : As above.   (Somnath Sarkar)
                        P. A. to Mayor

POLICY OF KMC ON

HAWKER ISSUES

Hon'ble Mayor of Kolkata has formed following two committees to adopt policy to control hawkers on the footpaths and carriageways within K.M.C. area on 05.06.2006.

❖ The committees are :-

1. **Apex committee at KMC level.**
2. **Apex committee at Borough level.**

❖ **Apex committee members:-**

Apex committee at KMC level

1. Member, Mayor-in-council(Roads & Engineering).- Chairman.
2. Member, Mayor-in-council(SWM & EWS).-Member.
3. Member, Mayor-in-council(Bustee & S.S.E.P). -Member.
4. Commissioner of Police, Kolkata.- Member.
5. Dy.Commissioner of Police, Traffic department. – Member.
6. 18 hawker unions – Members.

Apex committee at Borough level

1. Borough Chairman. - Chairman.
2. Officer in-charge of Police station.- Member.
3. Representative of Traffic department of respective area. – Member.
4. Representatives of different hawker unions.- Members.

After several discussions, the Hon'ble Mayor and Apex Committee decided the following hawker policy for the city of Kolkata.

- No hawker would be allowed to encroach carriageway.
- No hawker would be allowed on the footpath of width less than 3 to 4 feet.
- No hawker would be allowed within 50 feet of the road crossings.
- $2/3^{rd}$ width of the footpath to be kept open for movement of the pedestrian and hawking would be restricted within $1/3^{rd}$ width of the footpath subject to the width of the footpath and need of the pedestrian movement.
- Hawkers have to use kiosk measuring 5' X 3' maximum.
- No polythene cover, permanent structure etc. would be allowed on footpath.
- Hawkers are not to be allowed around the hospitals.
- A decision would be taken later on for issuing identity cards to hawkers to restrict hawker infiltration afresh.
- In case of any violation of the policy decisions, Police and KMC will be at liberty to seize all goods of hawkers from footpath and carriageway.

- One dependable NGO to be engaged for silent survey in compiling data in details about hawkers.

To implement the policy K.M.C. has taken several actions which are as follows :-

➤ KMC has taken up the work of demarcation of footpath to earmark the hawking zone at Brabourne Rd., Canning St., Kalakar St., M.G.Rd., K.K.Tagore St., N.S.Rd., Strand Rd., AJC Bose Rd., Rabindra Sarani, APC Rd., Aurabinda Sarani, C.R.Avn., J.M.Avn., J.L.Nehru Rd., B.T.Rd., Gariahat Rd., R.B.Avn., S.P.M.Rd.

➤ The KMC, in the mean time, issued a notice and published the same in different new papers drawing attention of all the shop owners to keep the footpaths encroachment free for easy movement of the pedestrians and failing comply with the same will draw penal measures against the offenders.

➤ K.M.C. has conducted several drives against unauthorized encroachments by hawkers and shop keepers jointly with Kolkata Police on the following dates: -

18.08.06, 22.08.06, 29.08.06, 24.11.06, 27.11.06, 30.11.06, 01.12.06, 15.12.06, 16.12.06, 18.12.06, 20.12.06, 21.12.06, 23.12.06, 26.12.06,28.12.06, 04.01.07, 06.01.07, 08.01.07, 10.07.07, 12.01.07, ·15.01.07, 17.01.07, 19.01.07,23.02.07, 24.02.07, 27.02.07, 28.02.07, 06.03.07, 07.03.07, 10.03.07, 13.03.07, 05.04.07, 07.04.07, 16.04.07, 21.04.07, 24.04.07, 28.04.07, 30.04.07, 14.09.07, 15.09.07, 17.09.07, 19.09.07, 20.09.07, 21.09.07, 14.12.07, 17.12.07, 18.12.07, 24.12.07, 26.12.07, 28.12.07, 29.12.07, 02.01.2008, 03.01.2006, 08.01.2008, 12.01.2008 and similar drives for removal of encroachment by hawkers will continue.

During the process of implementation of hawker policy several questions /points were raised from different corners and the members of apex committee accordingly revisited the whole thing and has taken the following decisions.

1. No hawker will be allowed within 50 feet of the 58 important road crossings. In case of any violation hawker concerned will be arrested.

2. No hawker will be allowed within 10 feet from main gate of schools and colleges.

3. No hawker will be allowed on the adjacent footpaths of main entrance of hospitals - except vendors who sell fruits and potable water for patients.

4. No hawker will be allowed in front of the big Nursing Homes like Bellevue, Woodland and Devine etc. etc.

5. Hawkers will not be allowed in front of the Central and State Government buildings/institutions/offices nor they be allowed on the opposite side.

6. Hotels running encroaching public places are to be removed by hawker unions.

7. The list of important crossings presented by Addl. C.P. (Traffic) will be compared with the list presented by hawker unions and decisions on uncommon crossings will be taken later.

8. Structures will not be allowed on footpath and carriageway. If found, will be demolished.

9. Hawkers along the wall keeping the front side free will use footpaths having wall at behind.

10. No hawkers will be allowed in front of heritage buildings. Hawker unions will organize / control the issue after discussions among themselves.

11. No hawking will be allowed within the places where imposition of Section 144 is in force.

12. Implementation of hawker policy already taken by apex committee is the responsibility of all the hawker unions. KMC and police authority will take appropriate course of action where the unions will fail to implement the policy.

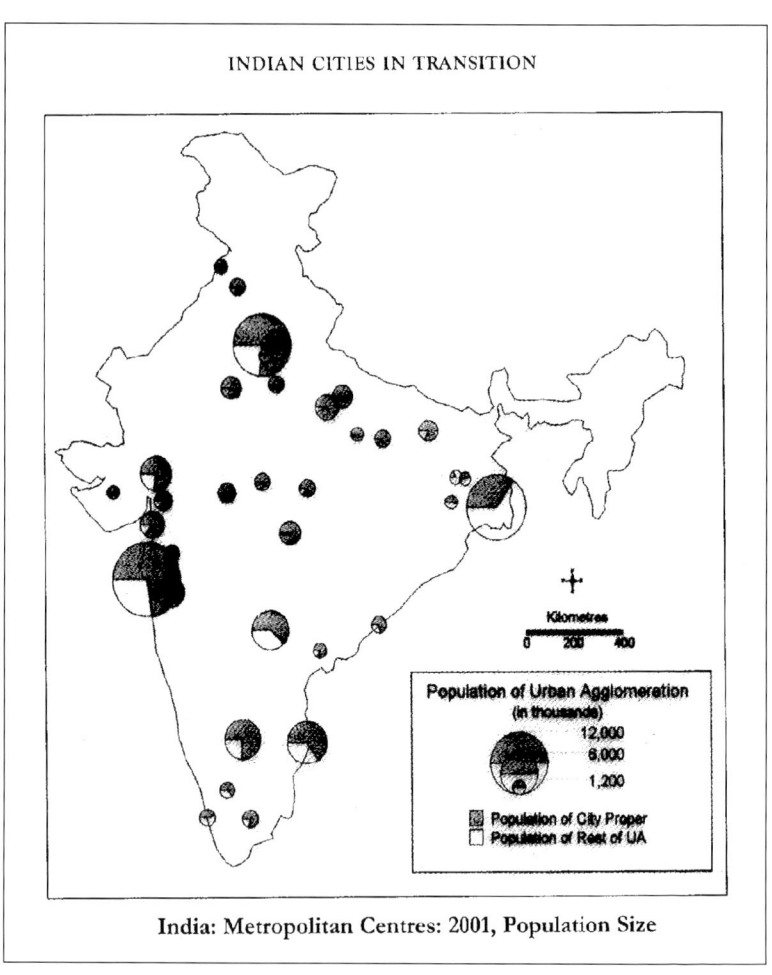

From: Shaw, Annapurna (ed.), *Indian Cities in Transition*,
Chennai 2007, p62

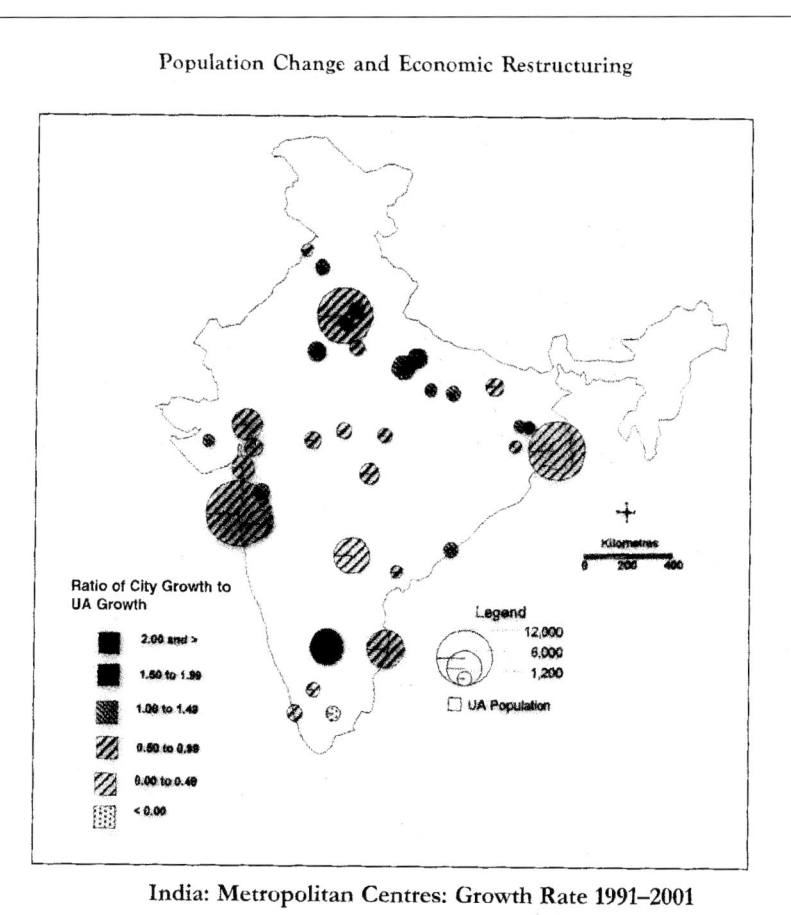

Population Change and Economic Restructuring

Ratio of City Growth to UA Growth

- 2.00 and >
- 1.50 to 1.99
- 1.00 to 1.49
- 0.50 to 0.99
- 0.00 to 0.49
- < 0.00

Legend

- 12,000
- 6,000
- 1,200

UA Population

Kilometres
0   200   400

India: Metropolitan Centres: Growth Rate 1991–2001

ibid. p63

The Growth of Calcutta in the Twentieth Century

Relative Placement of Tracts in the Growth of Population in the Calcutta Urban Agglomeration, 1901–81

Tracts		1901	1911	1921	1931	1941	1951	1961	1971	1981
Calcutta City	(a)	934	1016	1053	1165	2167	2698	2927	3149	3305
	(b)	100	109	113	125	232	289	313	337	354
	(c)	61.9	58.2	55.9	54.5	59.8	57.8	48.9	42.4	35.9
Surrounding Municipal Towns listed in Table 1	(a)	276	326	352	410	664	860	1208	1541	1809
	(b)	100	118	128	149	241	312	438	558	655
	(c)	18.3	18.7	18.7	19.2	18.3	18.4	20.2	20.8	19.7
Rest of the CUA	(a)	300	403	480	564	790	1112	1849	2730	4080
	(b)	100	134	160	188	263	371	616	910	1360
	(c)	19.9	23.1	25.5	26.4	21.8	23.8	30.9	36.8	44.4
CUA as a whole	(a)	1510	1745	1885	2139	3621	4670	5984	7420	9194
	(b)	100	116	125	142	243	309	396	491	609
	(c)	100	100	100	100	100	100	100	100	100

Notes : (a) Absolute population in thousands adjusted for boundaries
(b) Index Number of (a) with 1901 as base of 100
(c) Share of the tract in the population of the CUA in ratio percentum

From: Chaudhuri, Sukanta (ed.), *Calcutta. The Living City*, New Delhi 2005, p7

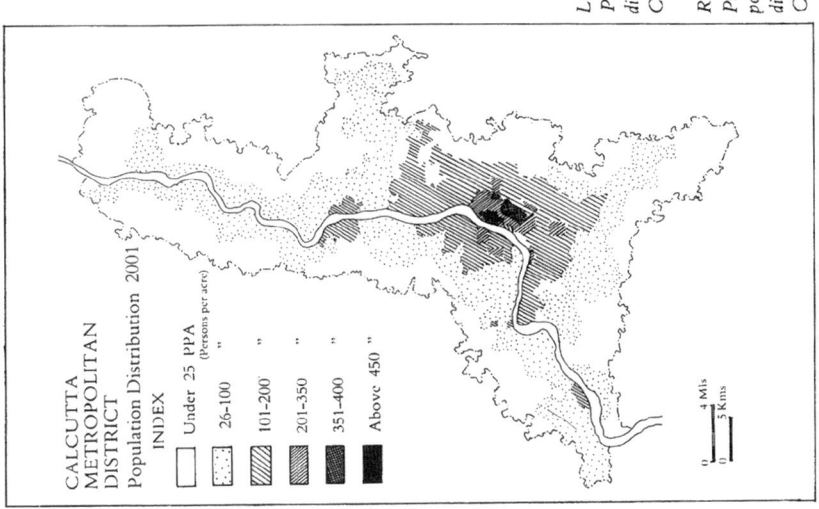

CALCUTTA
METROPOLITAN
DISTRICT

Population Distribution 1981

INDEX

Under 25 PPA
(Persons per acre)
26-100 "
101-250 "
251-450 "
Above 450 "

4 Mls
5 Kms

CALCUTTA
METROPOLITAN
DISTRICT

Population Distribution 2001

INDEX

Under 25 PPA
(Persons per acre)
26-100 "
101-200 "
201-350 "
351-400 "
Above 450 "

4 Mls
5 Kms

*Left :
Population
distribution :
CMD, 1981*

*Right :
Projected
population
distribution :
CMD, 2001*

ibid. p7

Map of the
Calcutta traffic network

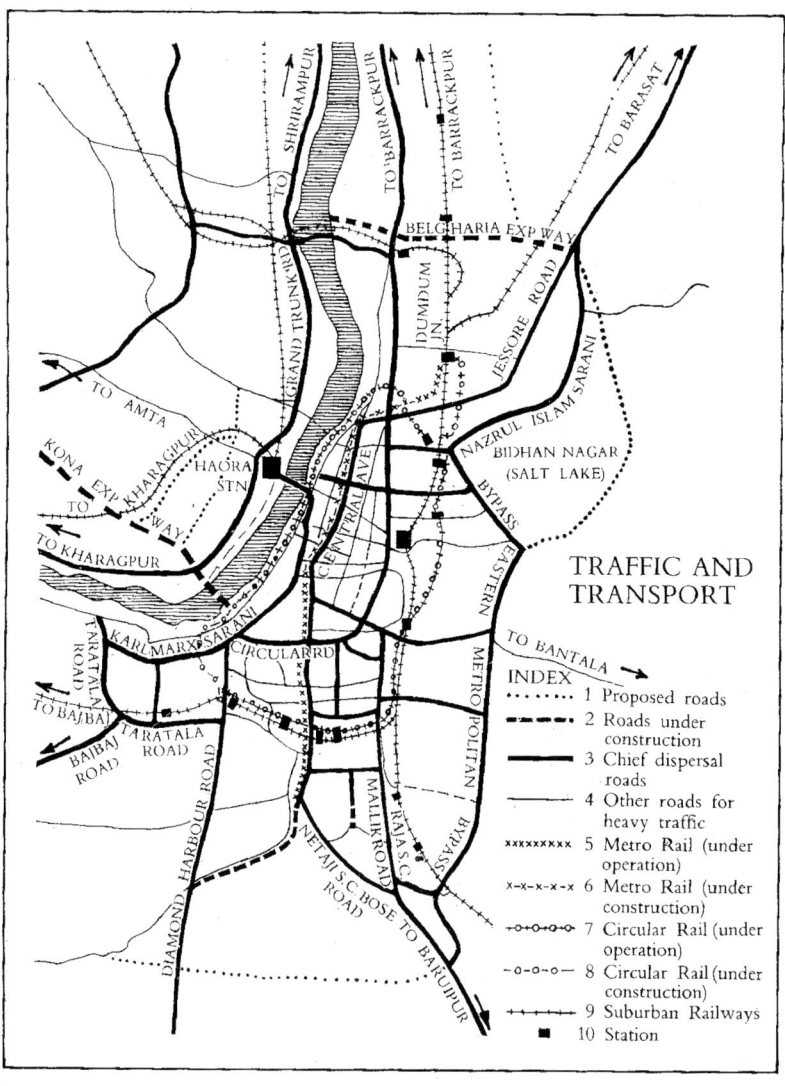

ibid. p154

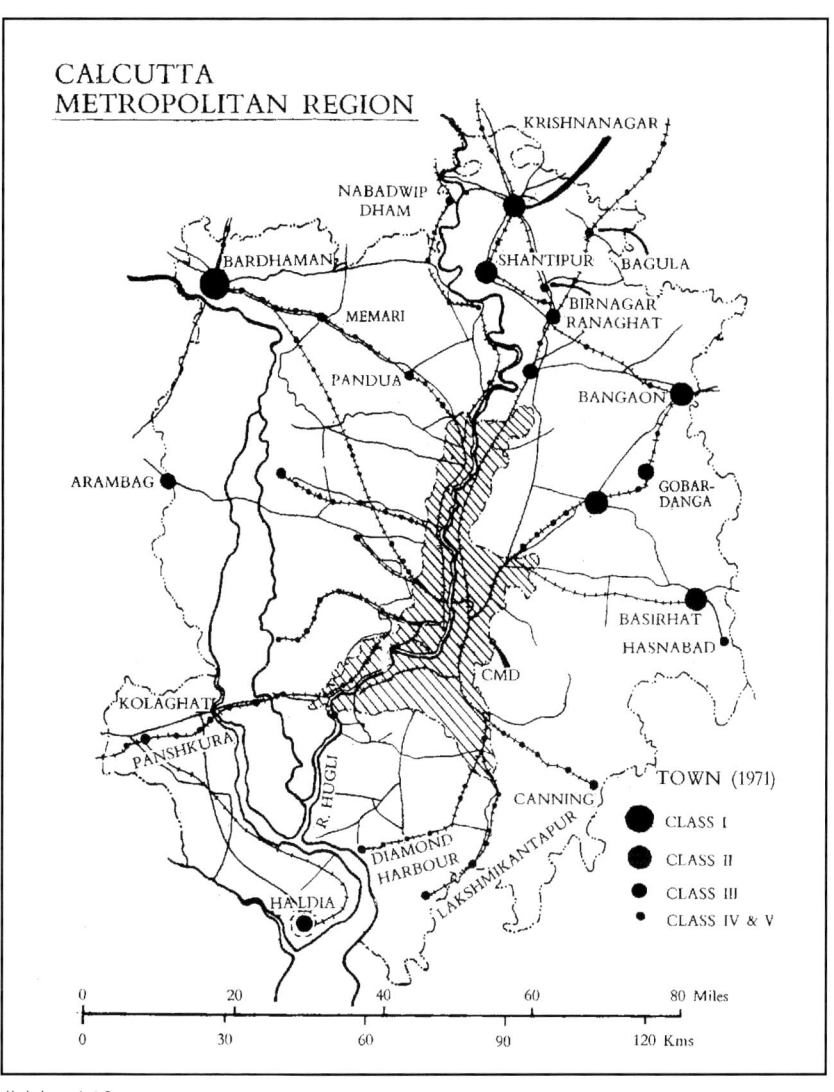

CALCUTTA METROPOLITAN REGION

KRISHNANAGAR

NABADWIP DHAM

BARDHAMAN

SHANTIPUR   BAGULA

MEMARI

BIRNAGAR
RANAGHAT

PANDUA

BANGAON

ARAMBAG

GOBAR-
DANGA

BASIRHAT
HASNABAD

CMD

KOLAGHAT

PANSHKURA

CANNING

R. HUGLI

DIAMOND
HARBOUR

LAKSHMIKANTAPUR

HALDIA

TOWN (1971)

CLASS I

CLASS II

CLASS III

CLASS IV & V

| 0 | 20 | | 40 | | 60 | | 80 Miles |

| 0 | 30 | | 60 | | 90 | | 120 Kms |

ibid. p146

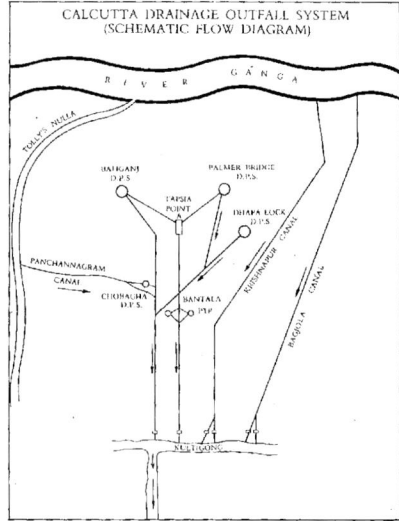

trips per day, crew size and tonnage collected per trip.

Diagram of the
drainage outfall system

2. Optimal routing and scheduling of the vehicles.
3. Improved repairing and maintenance of vehicles and equipment, to ensure the lowest possible operating cost in relation to the amount of refuse collected.
4. Sound personnel management and correct monitoring and field reporting of the removal operations.

Let us consider the problem in more concrete terms. Calcutta's streets are cluttered with refuse owing to indiscriminate throwing of waste, indicating a general lack of public awareness; also owing to roadside stalls and pavement habitations. There are over a hundred markets in the city which contribute 450 to 500 metric tons of solid waste a day. During the rains, the refuse chokes the gully pits, preventing the water from draining away. The practice of watering the streets to clean them has long been discontinued. So in good measure has the house-to-house collection of garbage, though it is understood that the Corporation plans to re-introduce this, ward by ward, as far as practicable.

The Corporation has also carried out some other improvements. Pay-loaders now operate to clear roadside vats swiftly and efficiently. Some vats have been replaced by containers,

ibid. p171

Encroachment of pavements: The number of hawkers in the area has increased at a galloping rate. According to the civic conservancy department's estimate, the numbers have more than doubled than what they were previous to Operation Sunshine. After Gariahat Market, this is the place where all types of garments and accessories are available. Pedestrians are forced to walk on the carriageway because of hawkers on the pavements. To top it all, the chorus of hawkers surpasses the decibels for noise pollution.

Residentspeak: There are no pavements in our area. The mayor has turned them into open-air markets. They made pavements with our money for us and then handed them over to the hawkers

for business. We can't walk on the pavements. Even while walking down the carriageway, the hawkers keep howling and try to draw our attention. Some of them even tease passers-by and a girl or woman cannot dare protest. Pro-hawker politicians say hawkers are poor people but we have our doubts. Because not a single square foot of pavement space can be used by a hawker without paying money to the political dadas. While they run their business on pavements, a good section of politicians also earn good money. — **Chandra Roy Chowdhury,** *social activist, 40A, Gariahat Road*

Councillorspeak: Encroachment of pavements by hawkers is not a problem for Bijon Setu area alone. In the interest of a handful of Left politicians, mayor Bikash Ranjan Bhattacharyya has shared people's pavements illegally with hawkers. A number of city-based politicians would starve if there were no hawkers. And they were the same politicians who had sabotaged the Left Front government's Operation Sunshine in the late 1990s. You will be surprised to know that pavements of Calcutta are being auctioned in districts of Bihar and Jharkhand. Some political leaders have regular agents there. Calcutta has six per cent road space which is 14 per cent less than the national benchmark. Now if pedestrians have to use them, the road space has to be increased by widening the carriageways. — **Rajib Deb,** *councillor, ward - 68*

Lost along the way

Prince Anwar Shah Road has followed the market's rules to change. For better or for worse? asks Sreyashi Dastidar

Between the Tipu Sultan mosque in the west and the Jadavpur police station in the east, a world lies utterly changed. An aerial view of Prince Anwar Shah Road captured ten years ago would be quite a different picture from one taken today. The face of the street has been under a cosmetic surgeon's scalpel, it seems — a plight similar to that of Elgin Road. But after such transformation, roads change their character more than human beings do.

There was a time not so long ago when, at the sound of the 9 am siren, hundreds of workers would walk down from all directions and troop into Joy Engineering Works, the manufacturers of Usha sewing machines and fans. Anwar Shah Road was very much an industrial stretch till about the early Eighties, with makeshift shops near the factory gates selling *saris*, childrenswear and household items. These would do brisk business in the first week of the month, which was also when the tea-stall owners went after the familiar creditors.

What used to be Joy Engineering Works is now the gigantic project called South City — an ensemble of sky-high residential towers, a school, a club and a shopping mall. The 9 am siren has long ceased to be a familiar sound of the city — perhaps in collusion with the vanishing industries. The labourers who raised South City did not need the siren, they worked days as well as nights.

Moving east from the sewing machine factory, there were three main landmarks (also stops for public buses): the Lord's Bakery (whose products have not seen the insides of shops in a long time), Dhaka Kalibari (like most religious sites, it shows no signs of losing popular appeal) and Navina cinema (once showing B-grade Hindi films, it only brings the top releases these days). There was also Jogesh Chandra Chaudhuri College. But without star-studded 'fests' or student-body elections marred by headline-making violence, it never became a presence.

This stretch now has at least three highrise apartment complexes, and the Princeton Club which has become the new address for 'rocking' young people. Dibyaroop Ghosh remembers being sent

The Usha factory: sepia tint

by his father to pay bills at the corporation office, where Princeton Club stands today. The swankier, more compact office is now cosily tucked inside the ground floor of the highrise that has come up in the former corporation premises. Ghosh also recalls a Charlie Chaplin festival at Navina cinema sometime in the mid-Eighties. "It is because of all the new complexes coming up in the area that the night show has been revived at Navina, and this can't be a bad thing," he says.

The Navina night show, the dense shrubbery beside the cinema, which doubled up as an illicit liquor den, and the tiny shops that always had a group of rowdies hanging around them were the unmentionables of Anwar Shah Road. But this was when the 'princes' of Prince Anwar Shah Road were Sheikh Binod and Sheikh Shahzada and their friends. Girls studying in Jadavpur University in the early Nineties would feel scared of taking the badly-lit Anwar Shah Road to go back to their homes in New Alipore or Behala after dark.

A little over ten years later, even the wild and rebellious sections of the road have faithfully followed the script of the market. A market culture, it is said, considers wealth-creation to be sacred, so the State must stand back and permit individuals to follow their self-interests. The State has been faithful to this dic-

tum too. It has not let principles of protection and benevolence come in the way of allowing individuals — a euphemism, no doubt, for cash-rich developers — to realize their self-interests. So a *jheel* may have to be sacrificed here, and a playground there, but only in the assumption that the market has its own mechanism to smooth out frayed edges.

Apologists for the market argue that over a thousand unemployed youth from the colonies around Gobindapur, Bijoygarh and Poddarnagar have found jobs in the South City mall and the other residential projects. Unemployment, after all, is the root of several evils, particularly crime. Santanu Ganguly, who has lived on Anwar Shah Road since 1985, says that law and order here have improved by leaps and bounds ever since the developments began. Besides, the Anwar Shah Road-Southern Avenue flyover has nearly halved his travelling time.

But some of the older residents remain unconvinced. They fear that soon their *paras* will disintegrate, since these are entities that rest on fragile arrangements of domestic and professional relationships, with their own social-moral structures and divisions of labour. Aurobindo Ghosh, who taught geology at Jadavpur University and has seen Anwar Shah Road when it was unmetalled, single-lane and unfit for buses, is seriously worried about the lack of long-term thinking involved in the developments along the road. Traffic is one of them. "But is anybody worried about the waste that will be generated by this road once all the residential complexes are full?" he asks. The developers are happy to leave worries of sewerage and sanitation to the civic authorites. But as more water bodies are choked, without any waste treatment plants planned, the problem slowly gets out of hand.

Figures show that in its power, reach and size, WalMart is bigger than Indonesia. The Sunday crowd at Spencer's Hyper at the South City mall seems to boast that the global reach of Spencer's will soon override the local identity of Prince Anwar Shah Road. Has a terrible beauty been born? The answer may only be found ten years later.

Rajeev Ranjan, a *satta* seller on Strand Road, is always ready to pack his wares and leave in the event of an anti-hawker raid by the Calcutta Municipal Corporation (CMC). But as soon as the officials leave, he sets up his shop at the same place. "This is my only livelihood and I cannot give it up," he says.

CMC recently gave an undertaking to the Calcutta High Court that it would take strict action against hawkers who ply their wares on important roads in the city. For thousands of street vendors in Calcutta, eviction is a fear they live with, and many like Ranjan are well prepared for the usual drill.

According to the National Association of Street Vendors of India (NASVD), Calcutta has around

ROADIES: Hawkers in the city may no longer have to live in fear of eviction

Bill of rights for vendors

1,50,000 street vendors. Ironically, Calcutta is the only city in the country to ban street vending. In 1997, the state legislature, through an amendment of the Calcutta Municipal Corporation Act, made hawking a cognizable and non-bailable offence, with imprisonment or fine or both. An overwhelming majority of hawkers in the municipal limits is unauthorised.

"Giving too much authority to the state and its enforcement agencies would in fact lead to illegal collection of rent from the vendors by the officials. We have seen that the illegal rent from hawkers and rickshaw pullers amounts to Rs 50 crore a day in Delhi. In Mumbai, rent from street vendors amounts to over Rs 400 crore a year," says Sharith K. Bhowmik, professor and dean of the School of Management and Labour Studies, Tata Institute of Social Sciences, Mumbai. Bhowmik was one of the members of the drafting committee of the National Policy for Street Vendors.

Like in other cities, it is likely that CMC officials and the police are

making money at the expense of street vendors in Calcutta.

Millions of vendors and hawkers across the country may have a reason to heave a sigh of relief if the central government's proposed Street Vendors (Protection of Livelihood and Regulation of Street Vending) Bill, 2007, becomes law. As the new Bill has various provisions that involve other ministries like home and labour, the ministry of housing and urban poverty alleviation, which will draft the Bill, has sought comments from them.

The new Bill aims to give street vendors legal status by formulating appropriate laws and providing legitimate hawking zones in urban development or zoning plans and ensuring their implementation. The new Bill would entail less intervention by the courts because of the uniformity of the law.

Street vendors across the country will also be brought under the social security net. Besides insurance, they will be able to get finance under the credit guarantee fund scheme for small industries.

Millions of vendors and hawkers will heave a sigh of relief if the Centre's proposed street vendors' bill gets on the statute books, says **V. Kumara Swamy**

The Bill is based on recommendations of the National Commission on Enterprises for Unorganised Sector (NCEUS), which was asked to improve upon the previous national policy formulated in 2004. After consultations with the nongovernmental organisations involved in the welfare of hawkers, street vendor organisations and others, the commission made some minor but significant changes to the policy.

The ministry has accepted al-

most all the recommendations and, in all probability, the policy will be tabled as a Bill in Parliament with some minor modifications, says a member of NCEUS. Once the Centre passes the Bill, the state governments and municipal authorities would have to carry out the necessary changes in the local laws within a year of the date of the policy's announcement.

Although the policy has found support from various quarters, it has its share of critics who say that it will not have much of an impact on the people on the street.

"One of the major weaknesses of the policy is that it treats all vendors as uniform and homogeneous. But that is not the case. The sector is diverse and the needs are varied," says Shrawan Kumar Acharya, professor, Centre for Environmental Planning and Technology (CEPT), Ahmedabad, and an urban policy expert who has written extensively on street vending.

But there are some departures from the 2004 policy. The proposed law does not limit the percentage of vendors in a town or a city. The earlier policy allowed a vending space of a maximum of 2.5 per cent of the total area of the town or city population. "I support the idea of not having a limit on the number of hawkers. Hawking works on the principle of demand and supply," says Acharya. But there are others who see a sinister motive behind this move.

"The government wants big malls and giant retail markets to develop. It does not see any role for hawkers. Therefore, by removing the restriction, it wants to virtually signal an end to hawking in urban

areas," says Shaikh Pervez, president, Urban Street Vendors Lok Seva Kendra, Mumbai. "It is an unwanted change. The percentage allotted for hawkers earlier was better," says Arbind Singh of NASVI, who was a member of the committee that drafted the new policy.

According to the new policy, town vending committees (TVCs) comprising municipal authorities, the police, and representatives of the street vendors or hawkers' associations will decide on the issue of licences and also on the number of vendors on each street. "Normally, it is the bureaucrats who decide about vending zones without having any knowledge of the actual ground situation, and hence it was decided that a committee involving different stakeholders would be more participatory and practical," says Singh. The decision on "no-vending zones" has also been left to the TVCs.

"Associations of residences, shop owners and other business organisations have not been represented in TVCs. This could cause problems as these bodies may try to stall implementation of the policy. If they are included in the TVCs, their resistance would be muted," says Bhowmik. On the fears of overcrowding on streets, Bhowmik says that TVCs can take a realistic view of street vendors. "One must remember that street vendors certainly do not want overcrowding on the streets as that would hamper their business. If vendors are regulated properly they will not crowd the pavements and cause inconvenience to pedestrians," he says.

"The policy focusses only on the needs of street vendors without any reference to public space management in cities and metropolis. TVCs have no local stake holders or guidelines to follow," says Neera Punj, convenor of CitiSpace, a Mumbai-based NGO fighting to keep open spaces from being encroached.

"A people-centric approach to traffic and transportation planning will automatically integrate the hawkers in the plan. We need a mobility plan and not a traffic plan. This aspect needs to be highlighted in the policy," says Acharya.

"We are so fed up with constant court orders and threatening postures by municipal authorities that any policy that gives us some relief from daily harassment is welcome, but I don't think the administration will let go of such an easy way of making money," says a member of the National Hawkers' Union, Calcutta.

From the other side of the wall

In the immense, tentacular streets of this city, reality is layered. There is the overt life of a street, and then there is that invisible reality — of lives that occur parallel to the ostensible, lives that are easily disregarded, places that have lost their value. It's been fifteen years since my family moved into our house on Prince Anwar Shah Road. Still I travel its secluded by-lanes trying to uncover the mystery that lies in its core.

Fifteen years ago, looking out of my study-room window was not as daunting as it is now. Like a pedestrian drawing in a school textbook, the façade of the Usha factory loomed large. The factory's quarters come with their own intrigue. You go to the end of what is a middle-class urban residential block, thinking you've come to a dead-end, and then, suddenly, there is this whole other world — single-storey houses, rundown shanties, a school — of whose existence there was no indicator until you turned that corner. I often wondered who these people were, living on my street but so very invisible, with their dwellings so vastly different from my own. The factory, in itself, was a mystery. Its very deadness, when placed against all the lives it supported, made it an object of childhood fascination. These days, my fascination with the view from my rooms is more Wordsworthian — like the little boy in *Prelude* who, sailing out in his stolen boat, came upon a jagged cliff which seemed to him monstrous at the time, and which, "As if with voluntary power instinct/ Upreared its head".

I have watched the birth of the proudest moment in this city's real estate development roster — South City. For days we have been haunted by the skeletal remains of the Usha factory whose sedated presence had been a source of strange comfort. The *kaashphool* on its fields has been replaced by colossal jib cranes, over 30-storeys high and with a fearsome life of their own. A new community of people is beginning to take shape. The wall that

Will the residents of South City ever know the pleasures of haggling at the local bazaar?

divides us shall remain, I'm told. The inhabitants of the four residential towers of this high-end housing address will not share our lifestyle. The children who will study at the school (with a world-class soccer pitch) within the South City complex will not have known what it is to ring the bell at the neighbourhood grocer's house in the middle of the afternoon and ask to buy a couple of lemons. In the neo-urban landscape of P.A.S. Road, they

will exist in their self-contained world of hypermarts and "multi-facility". In the sanitized environs of countertop-purchase units, they will never know the individual smells of spices and fish, and the theatre that plays itself out twice a day at the Lord's grocery market. What care would they have for the concept of haggling, what will they know of the joyous disgust of walking through the slush of a marketplace in the monsoons?

A particular social class is being excluded from this metropolitan redevelopment. Akash, the charming young tramp who lives in a shanty that has no water, looks at South City

with wonderment, but feels ill at ease inside it. The annual *mela* on the field beside the EEDF nursing home is more inviting. The open, carnivalesque spaces like the mela are giving way to segregated components of fun in, say, the upcoming Fame multiplex.

Outside the enclosed grounds of Usha/South City, Anwar Shah Road has continued its snaky meanderings and linked up with other roads — there is the new Lake Gardens flyover, and the newer connector from Jadavpur police station to the E.M. Bypass. At the Lord's Bakery More, competing *biriyani* stalls have taken up pavement space. A number of take-away eateries have mushroomed, probably to cater to the burgeoning number of students who come to the city from the Northeast — many of them study at Jadavpur University and live as paying guests in this area. The new Mainland China at South City mall will not find an able competitor in Hong Kong, the Chinese restaurant that has stood its ground for decades, almost right across the mall. The illegal motorworks garage through which one had to pass to enter my little residential lane has vanished, but a public toilet, with colourful murals on its walls and non-stop radio music for enhanced ablutionary pleasures, has come up. The Lord's Bazaar, the other entry point to my lane, keeps going round in circles, like an injured animal, every time the police serve the squatters eviction notices — a ritual conducted a couple of times or so in the past decade.

One wonders if the developers of this new modernity on P.A.S. Road are creating rapid changes, keeping in mind an equitable model for the redevelopment of public space. There is no one kind of 'public' on this street, but diverse pockets of people. While Akash visits the seedy eatery, Rayaaz, I go to the swank Princeton Club for its live music — both are indicators of the diversity of P.A.S. Road.

ROHINI CHAKI

Guess where we are? At Genexx Valley!
Our dream home is nearing completion.

Bickram Ghosh and Jaya Seal Ghosh

Genexx Valley is more than 60% complete. Soon, we'll be part of an exclusive neighbourhood. Already, over 1400 families have booked their dream homes. Including us. In a complex built by the reputed Paharpur Group. With the best of amenities. Genexx Valley. A home that doesn't stretch your pocket, only your imagination.

Project approved for Home Loans by all leading banks.	Architect: DULAL MUKHERJEE & ASSOCIATES

Homes from Rs.13 lakh onwards

● On D H Road, 15 mins from Tolly Metro ● 1200+ cottahs land ● 840+ cottahs open land ● 1875 flats in 33 blocks
● 2 to 3 bedroom flats from 811 to 1236 sq.ft. ● Huge playground ● Twin swimming pools ● Lakes with boating
● Residents' club ● Landscaped area ● Multi-facility gym

Marketed by

10A Rawdon Street, Kolkata-700017
Phone: 4002 5555, Fax: 4006 9000
E-mail: info@pioneerkhaitan.com

A project by

PAHARPUR COOLING TOWERS LTD.

Website: www.pioneerkhaitan.com
E-mail: genexxvalley@pioneerkhaitan.com

98300 66777, 98301 33777, 98300 39499, 4002 4002 or SMS PIO GV to 56767

An example of a real estate advertisement. The advertisement features a reputed tabla player and his film actor wife.

Acknowledgments

Thanks are first due to the Goethe-Institut for instituting the Artist-in-residence project at Max Mueller Bhavan its Kolkata centre; and for funding the outcome of the project: the film, *Kolkata Monodosis*, and this book.

Thanks to the many people who spent time talking with us, discussing the issues involved, and here members of the Hawker Sangram Committee are first on the list. Thanks as well to the many hawkers who gave up precious moments of their trading time to spend it with us. Mr Manish Chakraborty, architect and urban planner, is gratefully acknowledged for sharing his thoughts with us.

Thanks to the Kolkata Police, especially Mr Hari Rajan, the Additional Commissioner of Police at Lal Bazar, and to a Senior Officer at the Gariahat Police Station who wished to remain unnamed. Also wishing to remain unnamed was a Senior Officer at the Solid Waste Management department of the Kolkata Municipal Corporation. Our thanks to him as well as KMC for making information available to us at short notice.

Christopher thanks Mr Sanjoy Bose for the quick translation of a lot of German text into English.

Our thanks to Mr Debashish Chakraborty of Montaggio edit studio, and to Indrajit Das the editor for delivering the final version of the film in record time. Ms Ranu Ghosh and Sheik Abdul Rajjak contributed to this aspect in no mean measure. Similarly, thanks to Mr Barnendu Manna of Bits of Art for doing the same with the book.

Dr Reimar Volker, Director of Goethe-Institut Max Mueller Bhavan Kolkata, and Mr SV Raman, Deputy Director are gratefully acknowledged for their constant support.

We will not be able to adequately thank all these people and a host of anonymous support persons who contributed to a world record of sorts: the shooting, editing and exhibition of the *Kolkata Mondosis* film in two weeks, and a third week to edit, typeset and design this book.

And finally, without in any way diluting their splendid enthusiasm and encouragement, our thanks go out to the people of Kolkata. It was their active participation and extreme willingness to accept the normal strangeness of life which made this project so exciting, in what otherwise could have been a dull academic exercise.

Editor: Christopher Dell

www.christopher-dell.de

Texts: Christopher Dell, Patrick Ghose

Photography: Christopher Dell, Patrick Ghose

Assistance: Patrick SL Ghose, Kolkata

Book Design: Barnendu Manna, bits of art, Kolkata

Translation: Santanu Bose, Kolkata

Organisation: Dr. Reimar Volker, S V Raman, Goethe Institut Kolkata

Publisher: post editions, Rotterdam

www.post-editions.com

Coordination: Ruth Hommelsheim, Berlin

Videoclips: www.goethe.de/kolkata-monodosis

Research has been made possible with financial support of

Goethe Institut Munich, head of music department:

Jörg Süßenbach    GOETHE-INSTITUT

ISBN 978 94 6083 006 8